T0194806

The

SUCCESS
of FAILURE

The Discipleship of Jesus

RUBÉN I. CHACÓN

WESTBOW
PRESS*
A DIVISION OF THOMAS NELSON
& ZONDERVAN

WestBow Press books may be ordered through booksellers or by contacting:

WestBow Press
A Division of Thomas Nelson & Zondervan
1663 Liberty Drive
Bloomington, IN 47403
www.westbowpress.com
844-714-3454

ISBN: 978-1-6642-5924-9 (sc)
ISBN: 978-1-6642-5923-2 (e)

Library of Congress Control Number: 2022903707

Print information available on the last page.

WestBow Press rev. date: 04/29/2022

Translator's note on scripture usage

The original version of this book was written in Spanish, and quotes Spanish translations of the scriptures throughout, mostly from the Reina Valera family of translations. However, English translations do not always reflect the exact same word usage that the author highlights here. Thus, rather than choose one specific translation throughout the entire book, we have endeavored to find the nearest possible English translation for each occasion where the author cites scripture with a specific emphasis, to retain his intended meaning. We have added the common abbreviation for the version used, in brackets, following each direct scripture quote. The versions we have used are as follows:

AKJV American King James Version
NET   New English Translation
NIV   New International Version
NKJV New King James Version.
NLT   New Living Translation
RSV   Revised Standard Version
NASB New American Standard Bible

To all my dear brothers who, until today, have made defeat and failure their most frequent experience.

CONTENTS

FOREWORD

The term "discipleship" does not appear in the Holy Scriptures. Thus, it is not easy to define a biblical meaning that conveys the entire concept: the process, the methodology, and the objectives.

The word *discipleship* is derived from the Latin *Discipulâtus*, meaning: (1) exercise and quality of the disciple of a school; (2) doctrine, teaching, education; (3) group of adherents of a school or teacher.[1] However, these seem like definitions for nonsacred literature, and not very applicable to the school of discipleship that we see in Jesus's exemplary life.

In addition to the ambiguity caused by the absence of this word in the Bible, its usage has become ubiquitous in recent years, taking on different meanings depending on the context in which it is applied. Thus, it becomes even more challenging to formulate a definition that fits all cases. It means different things depending on where it is used. For some, it is a Bible study, for others, a group therapy session. For some, it is pastoral counseling, and for still others, it is a personal relationship between a spiritual guide and an individual (the "disciple") who submits to his guidance. Some focus on the process or methodology, while others look at the desired results, while yet others are more concerned about the content shared. In summary: there is much confusion in the church regarding this concept so frequently used yet so poorly understood.

Ignorance on the subject is further increased by converting our traditions and personal experiences into the source of revelation for the discipleship and the basis of our diagnosis. Today there is a very harmful practice regarding discipleship, which consists of the tendency to convert personal experiences and cultural norms into the basis and goals for the life-building process. This practice, which is as subjective as it is relative, adds another element of confusion and error to discipleship's already complex process. On applying this criterion, the final product is not a disciple made in the image of Christ, but one made in the image of the one who disciples him.

The picture becomes even more obscure when we also consider the various motivations observed in churches, as they incorporate "discipleship programs" to the already numerous programs that are drowning the lives of believers. What is supposedly life-giving becomes life-threatening. "We have to train leaders. Let's start a discipleship program!" "We need a commitment from our brothers. Let's do a discipleship program!". "We have to grow in number. Let's start with discipleship!" "We need more holiness in the lives of our members. Let's try a discipleship program!" Thus, discipleship becomes a program that, in the end, fails to produce the desired result, and ends up being unsustainable since it overwhelms and drowns, instead of giving life—abundant life.

But what does the Master say about this? After all, with his unsurpassed life and teachings, he remains the Master, especially in this matter of discipleship. Jesus is the Supreme Teacher. When consulting the Master regarding true discipleship, the problem arises when the clarification he gives us isn't always attractive, either to the world or to the church. Apart from not being attractive, it is difficult to understand the answers that he offers to our inquiries with astonishing frequency. For example: "Happy are those who weep." If one cries, unless it is due to intense joy, it is not because one is happy! "Happy is he who does not know where he is going to get money to eat." "Happy is he who has everyone against him." "Whoever wants to save their life will lose it." "Go, sell your possessions, give the money to the poor, and then follow me." Such words make no sense the first time one reads them, nor on the second reading either because the human mind cannot comprehend the things of the Spirit. Without the Holy Spirit's guidance, the words of the Master often leave one bemused or perplexed or both.

It is even more incomprehensible if one considers that the requirement, the path, and the goal of true discipleship is the cross. Death: emptying, giving up all partisan and personal understanding, recognizing human inability—its total inability to do something divine, heavenly, spiritual, of God. This is hard to understand and hard to do, especially amid the humanistic worldview we are surrounded by today. The harsh reality is that even when considering all our sophistication, knowledge, and self-help, we don't possess enough insight to make us capable of leading our own lives, much less transforming the lives of others. We have neither the sufficient intellectual capacity to understand nor adequate power to do what only God can do in us. The sacred "I" must surrender to death so that the divine Master can quietly work from the inside.

The text you have in your hands will likely cause you some discomfort at the first reading. However, more in-depth analysis with careful meditation will show you that it is necessary to go through the same process that the first disciples experienced: failure, waiting, and victory. Someone who wants to reach the satisfaction of victory without savoring the despair of failure and the uncertainty of waiting will try to achieve victory with his or her human strength and understanding. This shortcut produces total, absolute, and irremediable failure.

Such was my own experience. For years, I tried to understand and do God's will, with a sincere heart, sometimes with great effort and sometimes with little, with an ill-fated result. Upon realizing the depravity in which I lived, and the helplessness produced by not being able to do something about it, I experienced disappointment, discouragement, despair, and, finally, depression. Failure had done its holy and glorious work. The wait for the real resolution that followed failure, even though it was short in chronological terms, felt like a long period due to my internal suffering.

But God, who is rich in mercy and who loves us with eternal love, sent one of his children into my life, a wise man, experienced in the Spirit, one who loved discipleship and his Master deeply. This brother, who has since gone to be with the Lord, insisted that what I was missing was the person and the presence of the Holy Spirit. His first involvement in my life was not to apply a formal discipleship process or program—even though he was doing just that informally and indirectly—but rather to emphasize the imperative need to be soaked in and impacted by the Spirit of God. Indeed, he knew, because of his years of experience and revelation he had received from God that without the person, presence, and power of the Spirit, no discipleship process could have any positive effect on life.

The victorious life began the day the blessed Holy Spirit of God came into my life.

CONCLUSION

True discipleship remains the specialty of Jesus, produced in us by the Spirit of Christ. It is a process in which the disciple candidate is led to recognize his inability, his need, and his absolute dependence on God. He is then led through a wonderful transformation process, from the inside out, by the Spirit, assisted by the educational and formative ministry of the church, which consists of Christ, advising and teaching everyone in all wisdom, to present themselves mature in Christ.

May God bless all those who are hungry and thirsty, who are desirous to discover and live the process, content, and fruit of true discipleship—the discipleship of Jesus, those who are willing to go through failure, waiting to find victory.

—Jerold B. Keeling
Language instructor and translator
Missionary/pastor/teacher in North America, Europe, and South America; last forty-four years serving in Chile, South America

PREFACE

In a book that addresses the issue of Christian discipleship, you probably wouldn't expect to find a statement that the very first lesson every disciple should experience in following his Lord is failure. Indeed, every book on discipleship is supposed to teach you how to grow, develop, and achieve a victorious life, not to firstly show the importance of failing. Well, the thesis of this book postulates precisely this. Failure is not only the first lesson that every disciple must experience in following Christ, but it is the fundamental and absolutely necessary lesson for a victorious life. Without it, it is impossible to grow or win.

Likewise, you might be surprised to see that the second big lesson that every disciple must experience in his or her life is to wait. Probably this isn't what you expected to hear either! Failure should be followed by fighting, striving, acting, obeying … but not by waiting. This is what we commonly think. That failure and waiting are the first and fundamental lessons of Christian discipleship is surely not what you expected to find.

However, not only will this be the thesis of this book, but the author postulates that it gives an exact account of the discipleship that Jesus practiced. It challenges us, therefore, to review and compare our discipleship models with that of our Lord. It invites us to rediscover the discipleship of Jesus to see if we have perhaps missed precisely the most important aspects. Indeed, Jesus did nothing but follow the same model that his heavenly Father used when he gave the law to the people of Israel.

INTRODUCTION

The Lord Jesus Christ spent all three and a half years of his ministry forming twelve men. It was a time of true and authentic discipleship. The Lord Jesus walked, ate, taught, worked miracles, slept, and appeared among them. He revealed himself to them in all his glory, wanting his disciples to know him intimately. He revealed to them the Father, his Word, and especially the gospel of the kingdom of God.

THE SPIRIT DID NOT DWELL IN THEM

For the disciples of the Lord, who were the receivers of his Word and the objects of his training, what concrete possibility could they possibly have for being able to take on and live the gospel of the kingdom? We know that the disciples did not receive the Holy Spirit until Pentecost (Acts 2) or, perhaps, as John records in his gospel, it was right after the resurrection, when he said to them: "Receive the Holy Spirit" (John 20:22).

Indeed, the Holy Spirit dwelt with the disciples, but as the Lord himself testifies, the Spirit did not dwell in them. The Holy Spirit dwelt, at that moment, only in Jesus Christ. He was the only temple of the Spirit. However, as Jesus dwelt with the disciples, the Spirit, who dwelt in him, also dwelt with them. But, strictly speaking, the Spirit did not dwell in them: Jesus promised that in the future, it would be in them (John 14:17).

Therefore, we repeat the question: What real possibility did the disciples have of embodying the Word they received from Jesus? According to some commentators, at that time the disciples were not yet truly converted and saved, because they did not have the Spirit and therefore, they could not have experienced regeneration or new birth. I don't know if it is necessary to go to such extremes, but there is no doubt that, until then, they had not experienced the Spirit dwelling in them.

THE ESTABLISHMENT OF THE KINGDOM

On the other hand, we understand that the Lord Jesus Christ had to establish the kingdom of God, regardless of the aptitudes of the disciples to embody it. God cannot change his demands by virtue of the human condition, since the reality of sin, typical of the fallen human nature, is not his responsibility. However, what was the point of Jesus revealing the gospel of the kingdom of God to people who were unable to live it? It is difficult to imagine that Jesus's only intention was to establish the truth, since, as apostle John says, that grace and truth came through Jesus Christ (John 1:17).

Christ brought not only truth, but also grace ... especially grace. Of course, truth had to be established among men, and not only did it have to be known, but also to be lived. The problem, however, was that the demands of the kingdom of God were divine, heavenly demands, while the disciples, on the other hand, lived in human and earthly conditions. For the fallen human nature, the demands of the kingdom are not ingrained. In essence, exposing the truths of the kingdom of God could give the disciples the vision of what they had to live and embody but not the power to do it.

NATURAL INABILITY

For example, did it make sense then that the Lord would ask and demand of his disciples that they fulfill the Sermon on the Mount? To get closer to a possible answer, we must first ask if the disciples, while listening to their teacher, were aware of their total inability to fulfill what they heard. As we will see later, the disciples were not fully aware of their true condition. In fact, man has never been aware of his true state. Man is blind, and the only possibility for him to get to know himself, is for God to reveal to him his condition. Discovering our total helplessness is a significant revelation. Until that time comes, we all respond to the divine demands just as the people of Israel did when the law was given to them: "We will do everything the Lord has said; we will obey" (Ex. 24:7 New International Version).

It is true that Paul says, "Now it is evident that no man is justified before God by the law" (Gal. 3:11 Revised Standard Version). This judgment is spiritual, and it does not imply that men have understood it from the beginning. On the contrary, many not only believed that they could keep the law but also thought that they were indeed keeping it. In fact, not only men like Saul of Tarsus or the rich young man presumed to keep the law, but also groups such as the Pharisees and the Essenes.

DIVINE EDUCATION

The confusion here is further compounded by the oh-so-logical idea, which is ever so prevalent in the Christian mentality, that if God demands something from humans, it must be because humans can fulfill it. Otherwise, how would God ask for something that humans cannot accomplish? But it is precisely in this supposed divine incoherence that we find the answer to the initial question we have asked ourselves: Did it make sense for Jesus to demanded heavenly conduct from sinful men? The answer is yes, definitely yes! Not because the Lord expected his disciples to fulfill his demands, but rather because his initial goal was for the disciples to clash again and again with his commandments, until they had experienced their total inability to fulfill them.

His methodology would be to allow one failure after another until his disciples were empty of themselves to then be filled with the life of the Risen One. This is the entire point. Jesus Christ did, indeed, bring God's grace to humankind, but for some reason that is not easy for us to understand, he did not begin by telling them about grace but rather by speaking truth.

Jesus Christ knew better than anyone that the only way to prepare the heart of humans to receive the grace of God was simply to make humans first experience their own absolute helplessness in keeping the truth. Hence the importance of Jesus showing himself before his disciples in all his glory and power, because only in this way could their total inability be discovered. Our self-assessment depends on whom we measure or compare ourselves against. As the saying goes: "In the land of the blind, the one-eyed man is king." If the disciples had only compared themselves to each other, some would have felt better than others. But, when facing Christ, who can remain standing?

A DEVASTATING PROCESS

Many of us, in total ignorance of reality, have envied the privileged opportunity that the first disciples of the Lord had, (i.e., being discipled directly by Jesus)! When we imagine that situation, we surround it with so much romanticism and mysticism that it is difficult not to exhale a "Wow!" However, nothing could be further from the truth. For the disciples, following Jesus was a terrible experience. Again and again, they felt that they were not up to his standards. Frequently they made fools of themselves and experienced many embarrassments. He was so different from them that they were gradually filled with fear and confusion.

Jesus often treated the disciples mercilessly and harshly, or at least it appeared that way. In essence, the discipleship process was a demolition job perpetuated on the disciples. The only thing that sustained and kept them from giving up the process was the undeniable and glorious fact that Jesus Christ "having loved his own who were in the world, he loved them to the end" (John 13:1 RSV). Here, "to the end" does not only mean that he loved them until the last day, but rather "to the extreme" (i.e., to giving his very life for them). Only Jesus's unconditional love for them prevented the disciples from abandoning their Master.

Join me, then, on this journey with Jesus, through the three and a half years of training, or rather destruction, to which his disciples were subjected, in what we might call a true school of discipleship. For this purpose, we will follow the gospel of Mark for the simple reason that Mark is the gospel that uses the strongest and most stark language when describing the reactions and feelings of the disciples.

1

FAILURE

In Mark's gospel, we find eighteen different experiences to which Jesus's disciples were exposed. These are true-life discipleship lessons in which, on the one hand, the disciples got to know Jesus Christ, and on the other, they got to know themselves.[2] Eighteen is the sum of 6 + 6 + 6, and six is the number for humankind. Three times six signifies that the experience has been sufficiently tested and classified as categorically proven.[3]

Each of these eighteen lessons demonstrates the impossibility of living the Christian life through human efforts alone. For example, in the first lesson, the Christian life is equated to navigating in a world full of storms. In the second, the Christian life requires being capable of providing for the needs of a hungry world. Later, the Christian life also calls for the ability to walk on the waters of life. Moreover, it means being able not only to hear but understand and discern, to comprehend the words of Jesus correctly, and thus obtain the spiritual benefits they produce.

From the incident between Peter with Jesus, we learn that the Christian life is also about living above human emotions. This aspect must be developed and lived out in the valley of human misery, sustained only by the vision of Christ's glory contemplated on the mountaintop. The Christian life was made possible by the death of Christ, which now demands that we follow him in his death if we wish to experience the real power of the Christian life.

The temptations of power and privilege (nepotism) greatly hinder the development of the Christian life, as do narrow-minded criteria, legalism, and sectarianism. The Christian life does not discriminate anyone, especially children.

The lessons of Gethsemane and the arrest of Jesus illustrate that the Christian life consists of following the Lamb wherever he goes, not just for his blessings and faithful promises.

Finally, the Christian life can, at times, be a paradox or a contradiction that shocks and offends us unexpectedly, such as when the disciples had to deal with the death of their Lord. Obviously, this confusion is a result of our limited understanding of human and divine processes.

FEAR INSTEAD OF FAITH

> That day when evening came, he said to his disciples, "Let us go over to the other side." Leaving the crowd behind, they took him along, just as he was, in the boat. There were also other boats with him. A furious squall came up, and the waves broke over the boat, so that it was nearly swamped. Jesus was in the stern, sleeping on a cushion. The disciples woke him and said to him, "Teacher, don't you care if we drown?" He got up, rebuked the wind and said to the waves, "Quiet! Be still!" Then the wind died down, and it was completely calm. He said to his disciples, "Why are you so afraid? Do you still have no faith?" They were terrified and asked each other, "Who is this? Even the wind and the waves obey him!" (Mark 4:35–41 NIV).

The first lesson, according to Mark's gospel, consisted of taking a boat ride with Jesus. There would be nothing unusual about this, except for the fierce storm that arose, which started filling the boat with water. Meanwhile, Jesus slept peacefully on a cushion in the stern of the boat. The calmness displayed by Jesus contrasts sharply with the despair of the disciples, who eventually can't withstand any more and awaken him.

The Greek text states that they didn't just awaken him, but also got him up. Then they said, "Don't you care that we are about to drown?" The question has a strange ring to it. It seems more like a reprimand than a plea.

Almost as if they were telling Jesus, "Don't you care what happens to us!" How many of us have had similar feelings, maybe more than once? Even if we didn't say it out loud, at least we have thought it, "Where are you, Lord? Why aren't you concerned about me? Don't you care what happens to me?"

The Lord immediately rebuked the wind and calmed the sea, "Quiet! Be still!" The wind stopped, and everything became very calm. But the best was yet to come. Looking at them, he said, "Why are you so afraid? Where's your faith?" In other words, the disciples should have experienced faith, not fear, but they were full of fear not faith. Their first failure led them to realize that they did not have the measure of faith needed to follow Jesus. Isn't this our own experience too? Indeed, the Christian life is equivalent to navigating a world of storms, and those storms require a firm and stable faith. But how many times have we shown, to our great shame, that instead of being full of faith, we are full of fear and don't have the faith we know we should have?

SENSITIVE BUT POWERLESS

The apostles gathered around Jesus and reported to him all they had done and taught. Then, because so many people were coming and going that they did not even have a chance to eat, he said to them, "Come with me by yourselves to a quiet place and get some rest." So, they went away by themselves in a boat to a solitary place. But many who saw them leaving recognized them and ran on foot from all the towns and got there ahead of them. When Jesus landed and saw a large crowd, he had compassion on them, because they were like sheep without a shepherd. So, he began teaching them many things. By this time, it was late in the day, so his disciples came to him." This is a remote place, they said, "and it's already very late. Send the people away so that they can go to the surrounding countryside and villages and buy themselves something to eat."

But he answered, "You give them something to eat."

They said to him, "That would take more than half a year's wages! Are we to go and spend that much on bread and give it to them to eat?"

"How many loaves do you have?" he asked. "Go and see."

When they found out, they said, "Five—and two fish."

Then Jesus directed them to have all the people sit down in groups on the green grass. So, they sat down in groups of hundreds and fifties. Taking the five loaves and the two fish and looking up to heaven, he gave thanks and broke the loaves. Then he gave them to his disciples to distribute to the people. He also divided the two fish among them all. They all ate and were satisfied, and the disciples picked up twelve basketfuls of broken pieces of bread and fish. The number of the men who had eaten was five thousand (Mark 6:30–44 NIV).

This is the second lesson that the disciples would have to learn with Jesus. With Jesus's decision to get away from people to rest a while, the disciples set sail again to a deserted place. The people, however, took note and followed them. The story says that not only did they follow on foot but also that they reached the other side first. When Jesus arrives at the shore, a large crowd is already waiting for him. Jesus is then moved with compassion for the people because he sees them as sheep without a shepherd and begins to teach them many things. What great sensitivity Jesus has!

The hours go by, and it is getting late. Suddenly, the disciples, also motivated by great sensitivity for the people, approach Jesus with an idea, "Send the people away to nearby places, so they can buy something to eat." It seems that this time the disciples have risen to the Lord's stature.

However, Jesus expects more from them than just sensitivity. He tells them, "You give them something to eat." It isn't a suggestion, but a command. And it's not just a command for them, but for us too. How terrible! The Lord expects us not only to feel compassion for people but also to provide for their needs. He expects that, perceiving people's hunger, we aren't just moved to compassion, but also to satisfy their hunger. That is the Lord's standard.

The disciples are stunned by the command. They don't quite know what to make of it. "Is he serious? Did we understand him correctly?" Then, in trying to make sure that they understood the command, and appealing to human logic, they ask, "So, what you are asking us to do is to buy six months' wages worth of bread, and give that to them for food?"

As in the previous experience, the disciples' question has a strange tone to it. It is almost as if they wanted to point out to the Lord the nonsense that he had just said and get him to reconsider. Obviously, the disciples did not have that much money,[4] and besides, there probably weren't even enough bakeries around to supply such a large quantity of bread. However, the Lord knows perfectly well what he has said and proceeds to multiply five loaves and two fish into enough food for around five thousand men.

How embarrassing for the disciples and for us too! We think we are good Christians because we are sensitive to human needs, but we show that we are utterly powerless when it comes to satisfying that need. How many times have we experienced that helplessness ourselves? Perhaps frequently, right? The Christian life, which is backed by divine and heavenly provisions, unfolds amid a hungry and needy world that challenges us not only to be sensitive to those needs but also to be able to meet them. But who can do that on their own?

PANIC INSTEAD OF CRYING OUT

Immediately Jesus made his disciples get into the boat and go on ahead of him to Bethsaida, while he dismissed the crowd. After leaving them, he went up on a mountainside to pray. Later that night, the boat was in the middle of the lake, and he was alone on land. He saw the disciples straining at the oars because the wind was against them. Shortly before dawn he went out to them, walking on the lake.

He was about to pass by them, but when they saw him walking on the lake, they thought he was a ghost. They cried out because they all saw him and were terrified. Immediately he spoke to them and said, "Take courage! It is I. Don't be afraid."

Then he climbed into the boat with them, and the wind died down. They were completely amazed, for they had not understood about the loaves; their hearts were hardened (Mark 6:45–52).

And so, we come to the third experience of the disciples with Jesus. Once the episode with the feeding of five thousand was over, Jesus sent his disciples on the boat to Bethsaida, while he dismissed the crowd. This time the disciples were alone. After the public had left, the Lord went up on the mountain to pray. Night fell on the disciples out in the middle of the Sea of Galilee.

Time passed, and the night advanced to the fourth watch.[5] Jesus looks down at his disciples from the mountain, and the story says that seeing them "straining at the oars" because the wind was against them, he went to them walking on the sea. The Greek text translated here as "straining" is actually "tormented," which indicates that the disciples were in desperate straits and genuinely feared for their lives. At this point, Mark's gospel uses a somewhat strange phrase. He says that Jesus's intention in going to them was to "pass them by." I have the impression that Jesus, who obviously wasn't playing around, and neither was he indifferent to their plight, intends to get the disciples to cry out to him with all their might amid their despair. It seems that this is the lesson that the Lord wants his disciples to learn. Not only them, but us, too. The Lord often allows us to run into adversity so that we learn to turn to him. In the middle of our problems, he passes by our side, so we cry out to him for help. That's all he is waiting for from us to respond.

But is that how they reacted? No, to their shame, it isn't! Because, when they saw him walking on water, they thought, "It's a ghost!" What? Do the disciples believe in ghosts? It seems amusing, but worst of all, they thought Jesus was a ghost! And instead of crying out, everyone started screaming in fear. The expression "they were terrified," in Greek is "they began to tremble." Very literally, the disciples' legs were shaking. The Lord immediately had to speak to them, "Take courage. It is I. don't be afraid." Then he climbed into the boat, and the wind died down.

Can you imagine the faces of the disciples after the scene they had just made? They probably didn't even dare to look at each other, let alone look at the Lord. They had confused Jesus with a ghost! How embarrassing! How sad it is that Jesus is just one heartfelt cry away, yet so often we don't turn to him! The disciples were stunned because, according to Mark, they had not yet understood about the loaves. They were slow learners. Just like us.

The Christian life involves figuratively walking on the waters of the oceans of this life. However, just as walking on water is impossible in the physical world, it is also impossible for human nature to walk on the waters of life. It's not just that it is merely difficult; it is impossible. So, what are we to do? Only somebody who has already walked on water can teach us to do the same.

HEARING BUT NOT UNDERSTANDING

Again, Jesus called the crowd to him and said, "Listen to me, everyone, and understand this. Nothing outside a person can defile them by going into them. Rather, it is what comes out of a person that defiles them."

After he had left the crowd and entered the house, his disciples asked him about this parable. "Are you so dull?" he asked. "Don't you see that nothing that enters a person from the outside can defile them? For it doesn't go into their heart but into their stomach, and then out of the body." (In saying this, Jesus declared all foods clean.) He went on: "What comes out of a person is what defiles them. For it is from within, out of a person's heart, that evil thoughts come—sexual immorality, theft, murder, adultery, greed, malice, deceit, lewdness, envy, slander, arrogance and folly. All these evils come from inside and defile a person" (Mark 7:14–23).

This would be the next lesson in the School of Christ. The scene opens with the Pharisees and some scribes criticizing the disciples of Jesus. The reason: They saw the disciples eating with unclean hands—that is, they had not washed their hands. Immediately, the Lord comes out in defense of his disciples, giving a remarkable demonstration of how the Pharisees and scribes invalidate God's word by keeping the traditions of men. One can only imagine how smug the disciples probably were feeling as their Master defended them—proud, happy, protected, saying a silent "amen" every time Jesus dealt a blow to their opponents. Finally, drawing the whole crowd's attention and urging them to hear and understand, he concludes categorically with a masterful truth, which to this day should be remembered: "Nothing that comes from outside a person can contaminate that person. Rather, what comes from within the person is what contaminates him." One can even imagine the disciples wanting to give the Lord a round of applause!

However, when they arrived home, the disciples asked him, "What did you mean with that parable?" Then the Lord replies, "Don't you understand either?"[6] It's as if the Lord is saying, "I can see how the others might not understand, but not you!" Once again, the disciples realize that they are not up to the expectations of their Master. They should have heard and understood what the Lord was saying, but that wasn't the case.

Not only did they fail to understand about the loaves, but they also didn't understand his words.[7]

But that's the Christian life. It requires knowing Jesus profoundly, not just to understand his words but also to know how to interpret and apply them correctly. The latter is more critical and even more challenging to achieve. Reaching this level, however, lies outside the scope of our impoverished and limited human capacity.

NOT EVEN ON THE SECOND CHANCE

During those days another large crowd gathered. Since they had nothing to eat, Jesus called his disciples to him and said, "I have compassion for these people; they have already been with me three days and have nothing to eat. If I send them home hungry, they will collapse on the way, because some of them have come a long distance."

His disciples answered, "But where in this remote place can anyone get enough bread to feed them?"

"How many loaves do you have?" Jesus asked.

"Seven, "they replied.

He told the crowd to sit down on the ground. When he had taken the seven loaves and given thanks, he broke them and gave them to his disciples to distribute to the people, and they did so. They had a few small fish as well; he gave thanks for them also and told the disciples to distribute them. The people ate and were satisfied. Afterward the disciples picked up seven basketfuls of broken pieces that were left over. About four thousand were present. After he had sent them away, he got into the boat with his disciples and went to the region of Dalmanutha (Mark 8:1–10).

Thus, we come to the fifth lesson that the disciples must learn on this painful but necessary path of getting to know themselves because of getting to know their Lord more and more. According to Mark 6:52, the disciples had not yet understood the episode of the loaves, so the Lord led them to repeat the experience. In our ignorance of human nature, most of us would probably expect that this time the disciples would understand and rise to the height of their Master. But did they?

This time the Lord takes the initiative, letting his disciples know about the people's situation. "They have nothing to eat." It seems that the disciples' response should be easy. But their response is both a surprise and a shock, "Where could someone find enough bread here in the desert?" It's likely that the Lord expected a different response from them, more like, "Okay. We'll feed them." But that wasn't the case. Not only do they deny being capable of feeding the people, but worse still, they denied that the Lord could do it! Even if their response had been, "Lord, you give them something to eat," that would have shown some progress in the disciples' training.

So, for the second time, Jesus multiplies the bread and miraculously feeds four thousand people in the desert. Blessed be our glorious Lord Jesus Christ!

THEY STILL DON'T UNDERSTAND

The disciples had forgotten to bring bread, except for one loaf they had with them in the boat. "Be careful," Jesus warned them." Watch out for the yeast of the Pharisees and that of Herod."

They discussed this with one another and said, "It is because we have no bread."

Aware of their discussion, Jesus asked them, "Why are you talking about having no bread? Do you still not see or understand? Are your hearts hardened? Do you have eyes but fail to see, and ears but fail to hear? And don't you remember? When I broke the five loaves for the five thousand, how many basketfuls of pieces did you pick up?"

"Twelve," they replied.

"And when I broke the seven loaves for the four thousand, how many basketfuls of pieces did you pick up?"

They answered, "Seven."

He said to them, "Do you still not understand?" (Mark 8:14–21).

This sixth lesson concludes the disciples' first cycle of experiences with their Master—our Lord Jesus Christ.[8] After the miraculous feeding of the four thousand, Jesus and his disciples embarked for the Dalmanutha region. There, the Lord had an argument with the Pharisees, who asked him to perform a sign from heaven to tempt him. Jesus, knowing the intentions of the Pharisees, flatly refused to do so, left them, and went back into the boat, setting off for the other shore. This episode was the third experience with Jesus on board a boat.

The disciples are worried. The reason: They had forgotten to bring bread and had only one loaf for the trip. Jesus, on the other hand, is also concerned, but not about bread. His mind is still focused on the discussion with the Pharisees and especially on their attitude. The Lord, concerned with his disciples' care and training, warns them to be on guard against the leaven of the Pharisees[9] and the leaven of Herod.[10]

Upon hearing the word *leaven*, the disciples think that Jesus is scolding them for having forgotten to bring bread. They then start arguing among themselves. "I told you to bring bread." "But you were in charge." "How could you forget?" This is a lose-lose situation! Jesus recognizes his disciples' confusion and begins to rebuke them harshly with a series of reproaches that constitute a whole summary of the entire series of six failures:

a. Why are you arguing about not bringing bread?
b. Do you still not realize that you lack understanding?
c. Are your hearts dull?
d. You have eyes, can't you see? You have ears, can't you hear?
e. Don't you remember? (The meaning of this question is: Are you not even able to remember? Do you have bad memories?)

The Lord then reminds them of the two occasions when he had multiplied bread. In other words, what Jesus is implying is that if he could feed five thousand with five loaves, and feed four thousand with seven loaves, then why would he not be able to provide for the twelve of them with only one loaf?

Jesus ends the rebuke with one last question:

f. How is it that you still don't understand?

Thus, the sixth lesson ends with six questions that clearly highlight the disciples' resounding failure in following their Master.

THE FAILURE OF HUMAN EMOTIONS

> He then began to teach them that the Son of Man must suffer many things and be rejected by the elders, the chief priests, and the teachers of the law, and that he must be killed and after three days rise again. He spoke plainly about this, and Peter took him aside and began to rebuke him. But when Jesus turned and looked at his disciples, he rebuked Peter. "Get behind me, Satan!" he said. "You do not have in mind the concerns of God, but merely human concerns." Then he called the crowd to him along with his disciples and said: "Whoever wants to be my disciple must deny themselves and take up their cross and follow me. For whoever wants to save their life will lose it, but whoever loses their life for me and for the gospel will save it." (Mark 8:31–35)

The scene just prior to this one provides the immediate context for this story in Mark's gospel, which shows the moment of greatest clarity that Jesus's disciples have had up to this point. Peter, speaking for the twelve and by revelation from the heavenly Father, has just confessed that Jesus is the Christ or the Messiah. Thus ends the first part of Mark's gospel, which was intended to reveal who the Messiah is. And indeed, just as Peter said, Jesus is the Messiah.

In the second part of the gospel (chapters 9–16), Mark will tell us what kind of Messiah Jesus is. In the first part, the question was: Who is the Messiah? In the second part, however, the question is: What kind of Messiah is Jesus? And the answer to this last question will be: The Messiah, Jesus, is the suffering servant of God.

Therefore, from this point on, Jesus begins to speak to them clearly and openly about his death, which must take place in Jerusalem. It is at this point that apostle Peter once again enters the scene. On the one hand, filled with satisfaction from the clarity of a moment ago, making him feel secure and self-confident, and on the other hand, moved by the great affection he feels for Jesus, Peter takes Jesus aside and begins to reprimand him for what he has just said about his impending death. The Greek word for "reprimand" is much stronger. It indicates that Peter began to "rebuke him." How does that strike you? Where did Peter get such nerve? I imagine Peter saying something like, "What do you mean you're going to die? How could you even think such a thing? Don't you know how much we love you?"

Then, turning to the rest of the disciples to get their attention, Jesus said to Peter, "Get out of my sight, Satan!" What? Had Peter suddenly become an enemy and adversary?[11] What's happening here? How is it possible that Peter can move so quickly from a moment of glory to a moment of darkness? From confession to confusion? We, too, are so much like Peter! Can you imagine what the other disciples must have thought of Peter and how Peter felt? What was wrong with what he said to merit such a harsh rebuke? And if there was something wrong, couldn't the Lord have at least valued the sincerity of his words?

How treacherous our emotions can be! Peter, with complete ignorance of the things of God, and governed only by his human emotions, was, in effect, telling his Master, "How could you even think of going to the cross to bring salvation to men? Why are you so concerned about others? Think of yourself! Consider your own well-being!"

To make sure nobody would think that this requirement was only for Christ and not for all of us, Jesus, calling to the people and to his disciples, said, "If anyone wishes to follow me, he must deny himself, take up his cross, and follow me." The reason for this is as tremendous as the stipulation itself. "For whoever wishes to save his life will lose it, but whoever loses his life because of me and the gospel will save it." From now on, following Christ takes on a new dimension for the disciples. Mark rightly says that when they went up to Jerusalem, Jesus walking ahead of them, the disciples were stunned and followed him in fear (10:32).

The Christian life requires "letting go" of our loved ones, releasing them to God's will; however, our human emotions pull us in the exact opposite direction, seeking to tie them to us. And who, on his own, can overcome this? It's hard, isn't it? In fact, it's not just difficult. It is impossible.

HASTE MAKES WASTE

After six days, Jesus took Peter, James, and John with him and led them up a high mountain, where they were all alone. There he was transfigured before them. His clothes became dazzling white, whiter than anyone in the world could bleach them. And there appeared before them Elijah and Moses, who were talking with Jesus. Peter said to Jesus, "Rabbi, it is good for us to be here. Let us put up three shelters—one for you, one for Moses, and one for Elijah." (He did not know what to say, they were so frightened.) Then a cloud appeared and covered them, and a voice came from the cloud: "This is my Son, whom I love. Listen to him!" Suddenly, when they looked around, they no longer saw anyone with them except Jesus. As they were coming down the mountain, Jesus gave them orders not to tell anyone what they had seen until the Son of Man had risen from the dead (Mark 9:2–9).

In this eighth experience of the disciples with the Lord, they will see God's kingdom coming (when it indeed comes) with power. According to Matthew, "They will see the Son of Man coming in his kingdom." That is to say, they will see the Messiah in advance, as it were, appearing in the power of his second coming. This vision balances out the previous experience of death. The meaning of this is that Jesus would die not due to weakness but voluntarily. Being aware of his power, therefore, would allow the disciples to find the source from which to draw the strength they would need to follow their Master, even unto death. Following Jesus on the path to death ultimately leads to participation with him in his glory and his power. "If we suffer with him, we will also reign with him."[12] This preview, so to speak, of the second coming of Christ we know as the transfiguration.

However, the mention of the number six in the phrase "six days later" already anticipates a new failure for the disciples. This time from Peter, James, and John. When Peter saw Jesus transfigured and conversing with Moses and Elijah, he quickly rushed to suggest, "Why don't we make three shelters and stay here?" Then the writer clarifies that Peter spoke like this "because he didn't know what he was saying." The sense is that he didn't really know what to say. But who told him he had to rush in and say anything at all? Mark clarifies that the reason for his haste was because they were terrified by the vision.

In the previous lesson, the disciples had seen themselves walking with Jesus toward his death. Now, they are in glory. Peter rightly says, "Teacher, it's so wonderful for us to be here!" Who would have wanted to come down from glory and walk toward death? All of us would have liked to stay there. But the transfiguration is just a preview, the purpose of which is to prepare us to take the path toward the cross, and not to stay where we are.

Peter's haste was then interrupted[13] by the Father's voice, speaking from a cloud, "This is my Son, whom I love. Listen to him!" In his haste to speak, Peter had elevated Moses and Elijah to nothing less than the same height as Jesus. Thus, the Father adds, "listen to him.". It is not time to hear from Moses nor Elijah. The law and the prophets now give way to Jesus, the fulfillment of everything that had already been said by Moses and the prophets. As a result of the Father's words, Moses and Elijah disappear from the scene, and only Jesus remains with the disciples.

In reality, Peter didn't know what he was saying. Indeed, haste produces errors. We must be quick to listen but slow to speak.[14] But who by his own efforts can control his tongue? James rightly says: "For we all stumble in many ways. If anyone does not stumble in what he says, he is a perfect man, able to bridle the whole body as well" (3:2). So, it's just a matter of trying, isn't it? No, unfortunately not. All our human efforts will never be enough.

LACK OF PRAYER

When they came to the other disciples, they saw a large crowd around them and the teachers of the law arguing with them. As soon as all the people saw Jesus, they were overwhelmed with wonder and ran to greet him.

"What are you arguing with them about?" he asked.

A man in the crowd answered, "Teacher, I brought you my son, who is possessed by a spirit that has robbed him of speech. Whenever it seizes him, it throws him to the ground. He foams at the mouth, gnashes his teeth and becomes rigid. I asked your disciples to drive out the spirit, but they could not."

"You unbelieving generation, "Jesus replied. "How long shall I stay with you? How long shall I put up with you? Bring the boy to me" (Mark 9:14–19).

When Jesus came down from the mountain with the three disciples, he found the other nine disciples engaged in an argument with some scribes, surrounded by a crowd of people. What was happening? A father had brought his demon-possessed son to Jesus, but his disciples could not liberate him. No wonder Peter, James, and John didn't want to go back down to the valley!

Jesus then exclaims: "Oh, you faithless generation! How long will I have to stay with you?" We know that he had to stay with men until he could make their faith possible through his salvation. Until that happened, he had to keep on putting up with all of them, especially with his own disciples. Jesus then frees the boy from demon possession. Once they had arrived home, the disciples ask the big question: "Why couldn't we drive out the demon?"

"Because this kind of demon," said Jesus, "will not come out with anything except prayer."

This time, the disciples' failure is due to the lack of prayer. Jesus was a man of prayer, but his disciples were not. Compared to the Master's stature, the disciples once again had fallen short.

The Christian life is victorious because it takes place in an atmosphere of permanent prayer. Prayer puts us in touch with as well as in communion with the author of life, from whom we receive supernatural life—his life. This life enables us to navigate faithfully through the storm, feed a needy world, walk on water, understand the words of Jesus, transcend our emotions, control our tongue, and free the oppressed. We all know this, but most of us either do not pray, or we have a very poor prayer life. We have a beautiful theology of prayer but don't a praxis. We know that we must pray; nevertheless, we do not pray. We know that praying brings spiritual benefit, yet we don't pray. We know that one cannot live the Christian life without prayer, yet we fail to pray.

So, what's the explanation for our incoherent behavior? The answer is simple but painful: Over confidence in ourselves. In this light, prayer is only a practical reality when it becomes a necessity, when we realize that, apart from him, we can do nothing, and that whatever we do without him is nothing. Until that moment comes, we will inevitably know only defeat, as there seems to be no other way for us to realize that we suffer from absolute impotence when trying to live up to the Master's standard.

The Christian life demands that we descend permanently into the valley of need. However, the necessities we encounter there are of such magnitude that, without a living and personal relationship with the Savior through prayer, we have no chance of confronting them successfully. In short, descending into the valley requires the prior experience of having climbed the mountain.

FEAR OF FAILING AGAIN

They left that place and passed through Galilee. Jesus did not want anyone to know where they were, because he was teaching his disciples. He said to them, "The Son of Man is going to be delivered into the hands of men. They will kill him, and after three days he will rise." But they did not understand what he meant and were afraid to ask him about it (Mark 9:30–32).

In this tenth lesson, the Lord tells his disciples of his approaching death for the second time. However, not only do they not understand Jesus's words about his death; they don't even want to ask him about it. "Everyone," says Mark, "was afraid to ask." Of course, after Peter's experience, nobody wants to run the risk. Nobody wants to be called "Satan."

On the other hand, it seems that the unsuccessful liberation of the demon-possessed boy described earlier had caused them to forget the experience of the transfiguration and had brought them back to square one in their understanding of Jesus's unambiguous words concerning his death. Due to their limited human understanding, the news of Jesus's death is so overwhelming for the disciples that they can't grasp it. They simply cannot assimilate the possible departure and loss of their Lord. No amount of reasoning makes it coherent. They are probably also wondering, "But what will we do without him? What will become of us if he dies?"

THE TEMPTATION OF POWER

They came to Capernaum. When he was in the house, he asked them, "What were you arguing about on the road?" But they kept quiet because on the way they had argued about who was the greatest. Sitting down, Jesus called the twelve and said, "Anyone who wants to be first must be the very last, and the servant of all." He took a little child whom he placed among them. Taking the child in his arms, he said to them, "Whoever welcomes one of these little children in my name welcomes me; and whoever welcomes me does not welcome me but the one who sent me" (Mark 9:33–37).

In reality, were the disciples so crestfallen and disappointed with the news of the death of their Lord? Let's look. In Capernaum, once they got home, Jesus asked them, "What were you discussing along the way?"

"But they kept quiet," says Mark, because on the way they had been talking about which of them was the greatest. Isn't that interesting! They were silent because, like a child who's been caught doing something wrong, they felt like they had been caught red-handed by the Lord. But what had brought about such a discussion in the first place? What caused it? Without a doubt, it was Jesus's words regarding his death. And, although Matthew says that these words greatly saddened his disciples, it appears that their sadness was not an obstacle that kept them from talking about who would be the successor, as Jesus walked on ahead of them.

The questions they were asking were not, "What will we do without him? What will happen to us when he dies?" No, they weren't asking the questions we might assume. Their questions were, "Since the Lord, according to his own declaration, is going to die, who among us will take his place? Who will take over the leadership of the group?" What a scene! On the one hand, they were speaking with faces full of sadness and voices broken with emotion, while simultaneously discussing who would be the successor. Have you ever seen a similar scene? I have. It resembles those people who start to fight over a relative's inheritance when he or she hasn't even died yet. How pathetic!

THE NARROW-MINDEDNESS OF THE DISCIPLES

"Teacher," said John, "we saw someone driving out demons in your name and we told him to stop, because he was not one of us."

"Do not stop him," Jesus said. "For no one who does a miracle in my name can in the next moment say anything bad about me, for whoever is not against us is for us. Truly I tell you, anyone who gives you a cup of water in my name because you belong to the Messiah will certainly not lose their reward" (Mark 9:38–41).

The twelfth lesson takes place within the previous scene. Perhaps what happened here is that, having been unveiled by the Lord, the disciples' shame must have been so great, especially in the case of John, that he couldn't find a better way out than to abruptly interrupt the Master and quickly change the subject. John is confident that what he is about to tell Jesus is so discerning and wise that it will somehow erase the mistake they had just made.

"Teacher," says John, "We saw a man who was casting out demons in your name, but he's not one of us, so we told him to stop." John must have looked forward to his Master's approval. They really wanted to experience the sensation of getting it right just once! Had they hit the mark this time?

Jesus replied, "Do not forbid it."

Today, we would respond with these arguments. "But he's not from our denomination!" "Do not forbid it."

"But he doesn't have our doctrine!" "Do not forbid it."

"But he's not from our ministry!" "Do not forbid it!"

Why? "Because no one who does a miracle in my name can quickly speak ill of me. Because he who is not against us is with us," said Jesus.

With this twelfth lesson, the second series of six experiences lived by the disciples while following the Lord comes to an end. In all these cases, the image of Jesus grows—becomes gigantic—while theirs decreases and shrinks. He becomes increasingly more glorious and wonderful; they, however, more opaque and carnal. The most important thing taking place in the disciples' lives is that while getting to know their Lord, they are getting to know themselves. This lesson will be fundamental in the future.

THE MISTAKE OF IGNORING CHILDREN

People were bringing little children to Jesus for him to place his hands on them, but the disciples rebuked them. When Jesus saw this, he was indignant. He said to them, "Let the little children come to me, and do not hinder them, for the kingdom of God belongs to such as these. Truly I tell you, anyone who will not receive the kingdom of God like a little child will never enter it." And he took the children in his arms, placed his hands on them, and blessed them (Mark 10:13–16).

This episode initiates the third and final series of six of Jesus's discipleship experiences with his disciples. How do we know? According to Luke, all the upcoming experiences are framed within the context of Jesus's final trip to Jerusalem,[15] this time to die. We can call this journey "the road to the cross," and it covers the last six months of Jesus's life.

People weren't just interested in listening to Jesus; they wanted to bring their children to him so he could touch them. What a beautiful and meaningful gesture by these parents! The disciples did not see it that way, however. On the contrary, they rebuked the people who brought the children. "This meeting is not for children." "Don't you know that children are a nuisance?" "They are the church of tomorrow; don't bring them today."

When Jesus realized what was happening, Mark says he was indignant. This is the only mention in the entire New Testament of Jesus in this state of mind.[16] This fact, on its own, indicates the great appreciation and affection that Jesus felt for the children, and how important they were to him. Therefore, he said to the disciples angrily, "Let the children come to me and do not forbid it!" The disciples not only wanted to prevent others who were not of their same "denomination" from ministering but also wanted to prevent children from coming to Christ. That's how we are! Narrow-minded!

Jesus ends his teaching by declaring that anyone who does not embrace God's kingdom as a child will not enter it. Immediately, laying his hands on them, he blessed them, but not without first taking them into his arms.

ONCE AGAIN, POWER IS AN UNRESOLVED ISSUE

Then James and John, the sons of Zebedee, came to him. "Teacher," they said, "we want you to do for us whatever we ask."

"What do you want me to do for you?" he asked.

They replied, "Let one of us sit at your right and the other at your left in your glory."

"You don't know what you are asking," Jesus said. "Can you drink the cup I drink or be baptized with the baptism I am baptized with?"

"We can," they answered.

Jesus said to them, "You will drink the cup I drink and be baptized with the baptism I am baptized with, but to sit at my right or left is not for me to grant. These places belong to those for whom they have been prepared."

When the ten heard about this, they became indignant with James and John. Jesus called them together and said, "You know that those who are regarded as rulers of the Gentiles lord it over them, and their high officials exercise authority over them. Not so with you. Instead, whoever wants to become great among you must be your servant, and whoever wants to be first must be slave of all. For even the Son of Man did not come to be served, but to serve, and to give his life as a ransom for many" (Mark 10:35–45).

Jesus's third mention of his impending death is the immediate context of this narrative, thus giving his disciples a new opportunity to demonstrate what they have learned. Remember that on the previous occasion, when Jesus told them about his death for the second time, even though they were afraid to ask him about it after what had happened to Peter, they still had no inhibitions about discussing among themselves who would be the greatest. But now they have a new opportunity. Surely, this time they won't want to take advantage of the situation for personal benefit. Let's look.

Right after the Lord finished speaking to the disciples regarding his death, James and John, the sons of Zebedee, approached him with a request: "Let one of us sit at your right and the other at your left in your glory." But where does this request originate? How does this relate to what

Jesus had just said about his death? The truth is there isn't any relationship, because the request by James and John does not arise from the words of Jesus about his death, but rather from his remarks concerning the rich young man. In that context, according to Matthew, Jesus had promised his disciples that, "at the renewal of all things, when the Son of Man sits on his glorious throne, you who have followed me will also sit on twelve thrones, judging the twelve tribes of Israel."[17] Hence, the request by the sons of Zebedee.

This idea of sitting on thrones with Jesus became a fixation for James and John, to the point that, ignoring Jesus's words about his death, they returned to the issue of participation in the Lord's glory. How tremendous this is! Jesus is talking about his death, and the disciples are thinking of places of privilege.

According to protocol, the person of the highest rank or dignity should sit in the center. From there, the others are seated outward to the right and the left, in descending order of honor. It is precisely this that James and John were requesting. With the Lord in the middle, they wanted to be seated one on the right and the other on the left. Perhaps Zebedee's sons felt entitled to the best positions because of the close family ties they probably had with Jesus.[18]

Jesus's response, however, was, "You don't know what you are asking." How many times have the disciples heard these same words from the Lord so far? Several times, right? They do not know what they are asking, because it is not the prerogative of Jesus to grant these privileged places. Only the Father can do that. Neither are the best places granted to those who ask for them, nor to those who think they are entitled to them, but to those prepared to participate in the cup and the baptism of his passion and death. To participate in his glory, one must first share the bitter cup of pain and the baptism of Jesus's suffering. Truly James and John had no idea what they were asking.

But that's not all. What about the other disciples? Was this desire for power and privilege only attributed to James and John? The text says that when the others heard about the request made by the sons of Zebedee, they were indignant with them.[19] Interesting, don't you think? They were outraged not because James and John had requested such a privilege, but because they had beat them to it!

The Christian life consists of oneself decreasing so that Christ can be lifted and exalted in the church and through the church. However, the world runs in an unbridled and crazy race not to fade away but rather to be exalted! It seeks to climb, doing "whatever it takes," even at the cost of knocking down or trampling on those who stand in the way. What is the reason for such a frantic struggle? Stated very simply, anyone who doesn't make it to the top is a nobody. This is the value system of the world. The world does not measure you for who you are, but for what you have. Your dignity depends on your position. If you do not have a high social status, you are a failure, a loser, a nobody. So, if you want to be recognized by society, you better work with all your strength to make the lyrics of this popular Spanish song the reason and purpose of your existence:

An entire existence to see myself become a good runner;
all my patience day by day to make me better and better.
To be third is to lose, being second is not the same as finishing first.
I'm going to win, I'm going to win; I'll die trying to get there …
I'm going to be able to prove it, I'm going to win …
So much sacrifice, so much rage, so long to see what I am.
What force pushes me and puts me in the lead of the competition?
To be third is to lose … a little more, a little more and I'll be the ace.

So cold, so calculating, so cruel and merciless is life in this world. But how starkly contrasting and powerful are the words of Jesus that we are called to live in the jungle of the survival of the fittest: "Whoever wants to become great among you must be your servant, and whoever wants to be first must be slave of all."

Who then can meet this huge challenge posed by the Christian life?

WHEN HE OFFENDS US

Jesus said to them: "All of you will be ashamed of me and leave me tonight. For it is written, 'I will kill the shepherd and the sheep of the flock will spread everywhere.' After I am raised from the dead, I will go before you into the country of Galilee."

Peter said to him, "Even if all men are ashamed of You and leave You, I never will." Jesus said to him, "For sure, I tell you, that today, even tonight, before a rooster crows two times, you will say three times you do not know Me." Peter spoke with strong words, "Even if I have to die with you, I will never say that I do not know you." All the followers said the same thing (Mark 14:26–31 New Living Translation).

This is the disciples' fifteenth experience in their relationship with the Lord, and perhaps the most difficult to overcome. Jesus is now in Jerusalem, where he has just celebrated the Passover feast with them. When they leave the city in the direction of the Mount of Olives, Jesus utters some terrible words. The phrase in Greek means, "You will all be offended by me," but literally says, "You will all stumble over me." How could Jesus offend and cause to stumble? This wasn't what they expected at all! But hasn't the Lord ever offended you? Has he never done something that made you stumble? In the disciples' case, after finally realizing that Jesus was the Messiah, it was too much to ask that they not stumble at the imminence of his death. "If he is the Messiah, then he cannot die; if he dies, he is not the Messiah." It's likely that is what the disciples were thinking. So, Jesus, aware of this, warns them that his death will trip them up. They won't be able to believe in him any longer.[20]

What? Is he really going to offend me? Surely this would be most difficult to accept. Anyone would think, "Impossible!" So, it's not surprising that Peter said, "Even if everyone else leaves, I will not. Even in the unlikely event that everyone else fails, I will not fail you." Peter's confidence in himself is absolute, despite the clear warning implicit in Jesus's words. This catches our attention. One would expect that at this stage of the process, following one failure after another, Peter would be more debilitated and not so self-confident. At the very least, one would expect that by this time, Peter would have realized that Jesus knows more than he, and that he knows what he's talking about. But unfortunately, that isn't the case.

Jesus, seeking to make Peter reconsider, warns him, "Truly I say to you that today, this very night before the rooster crows twice, you will deny me three times." It is as if Jesus were telling him, "Peter, Peter, don't contradict me. I know exactly what you will do tonight. Believe me." In the face of such clear and precise words expressed by the one who knows the disciples best, surely Peter would surrender and accept that his Master was right. But is that what he did? Amazingly not! With total ignorance of himself and even great zeal, he said, "Even if I have to die with you, I will never deny you." Only someone who doesn't know himself well could speak these words. Nevertheless, isn't that what all of us would say? If someone asked us, "Would you deny the Lord?" Wouldn't we all respond like Peter, "I will never deny you"? In my case, my thought is this: I may be a bad disciple, full of defects and inconsistencies, but to deny my Lord? Never!

All the other disciples said precisely the same.

The Christian life is not only filled with great victories and blessings but also with great paradoxes that almost always surpass our limited understanding, and which, for the same reason, must be endured almost entirely by way of resignation. It's even worse when these paradoxes come from the Lord himself. What can sustain us through this? The glorious fact that although God is light, he also dwells in darkness. He lives in the light, but he also lives in darkness.[21] In fact, the Son of God himself went through the darkest of nights for us. So, in following the Lord as his disciples, it is inevitable that we will also follow him through situations of this kind. The disciples "follow the Lamb wherever he goes."[22] Job, who knew about these experiences, says:

> He has blocked my way so I cannot pass; he has shrouded my paths in darkness (Job 19:8 NIV).

> Yet when I hoped for good, evil came; when I looked for light, then came darkness (Job 30:26 NIV).

However, on an encouraging note, let's say that our dark nights can never compare with Christ's. The dark night that Christ had to go through no mortal will ever have to experience. He died, abandoned by the Father, albeit he died trusting him. It would seem that if God abandons you, there is nothing else to do. However, in that same situation, Jesus still trusted and died, placing his hope in his Father. Hallelujah!

WHEN WE DISAPPOINT OTHERS

They went to a place called Gethsemane, and Jesus said to his disciples, "Sit here while I pray." He took Peter, James, and John along with him, and he began to be deeply distressed and troubled. "My soul is overwhelmed with sorrow to the point of death," he said to them. "Stay here and keep watch." Going a little farther, he fell to the ground and prayed that if possible, the hour might pass from him. "Abba, Father," he said, "everything is possible for you. Take this cup from me. Yet not what I will, but what you will."

Then he returned to his disciples and found them sleeping. "Simon," he said to Peter, "are you asleep? Couldn't you keep watch for one hour? Watch and pray so that you will not fall into temptation. The spirit is willing, but the flesh is weak." Once more he went away and prayed the same thing. When he came back, he again found them sleeping, because their eyes were heavy. They did not know what to say to him.

Returning the third time, he said to them, "Are you still sleeping and resting? Enough! The hour has come. Look, the Son of Man is delivered into the hands of sinners. Rise! Let us go! Here comes my betrayer (Mark 14:32–42 NIV).

This incident presents one of the saddest and most terrible moments that Jesus experienced. The journey to his death, to Jerusalem, had begun six months previously, and now the time has finally come. He needs to pray at this crucial moment. So, he goes with his disciples to Gethsemane's garden and, once there, tells them, "Sit here while I pray." His words are addressed to all his disciples except Peter, James, and John, whom he takes with him, leaving the rest of the group behind.

Jesus feels so alone, and, more than ever, he needs the company, friendship, and solidarity of his companions. What better way to face this moment, than surround himself with his three closest disciples? They are the ones who had accompanied him when he resurrected Jairus's daughter and the same three who had witnessed his transfiguration on the mountain. Few things are more precious than having close friends around you in times of difficulty.

The story goes on to say that Jesus "began to feel deeply distressed[23] and troubled."[24] As if seeking help from his friends, he tells them, "My soul is overwhelmed with sorrow to the point of death; stay here and keep watch." It's as if he is asking them, "Be with me, don't leave me alone. Help me get through this moment." And stepping away from the three, he began to pray.

But when he returned, he found them sleeping. What a disappointment! Jesus, who had always been there alongside his disciples, who was always there every time they needed him, now finds that they fail him on the only occasion when he needs them. What a terrible experience when your friends fail you when you need them most! But also, how awful to know that you failed your best friend when he needed you most! That's what the disciples must have been feeling.

The Master then says to Peter, "Didn't you even have the strength to keep watch for an hour?" How fragile, weak, and unfaithful human nature is! "Watch and pray," the Lord insists, turning away from them again to pray. When he returns a second time, he again finds Peter, James, and John, sleeping, "because their eyes were very heavy with sleep," and they were speechless. Once again, they have failed when given a second chance.

If that weren't already enough, this happens yet a third time. Only this time, the Lord has already resolved the situation, and despite his human frailty, he has chosen God's will. So, with a firm and determined voice, he says, "Get up, let's go!" And he went to meet the one who would betray him, the traitor.

NAKED AT THE MOMENT OF TRUTH

> Just as he was speaking, Judas, one of the twelve, appeared. With him was a crowd armed with swords and clubs, sent from the chief priests, the teachers of the law, and the elders. Now the betrayer had arranged a signal with them, "The one I kiss is the man; arrest him and lead him away under guard." Going at once to Jesus, Judas said, "Rabbi!" and kissed him. The men seized Jesus and arrested him. Then one of those standing near drew his sword and struck the servant of the high priest, cutting off his ear.

"Am I leading a rebellion," said Jesus, "that you have come out with swords and clubs to capture me? Every day I was with you, teaching in the temple courts, and you did not arrest me. But the Scriptures must be fulfilled." Then everyone deserted him and fled (Mark 14:43–50 NIV).

This experience, the next to the last that Jesus's disciples will go through, is the seventeenth failure in their attempt to rise to the level that their Master expected of them.

Jesus had not even finished talking to his disciples when Judas appeared, along with a crowd of people equipped with swords and clubs, to arrest the Lord and take him before the high priest. Judas is the only one in the crowd who knows Jesus, but he had given a sign by which to identify him: "The one I kiss, that's he." Indeed, Judas approached Jesus and said, "Rabbi," then kissed him. The crowd seized him.

Immediately, in a way we wouldn't expect, Peter bursts into the scene, unsheathing his sword, and cuts off the ear of the high priest's servant. Peter was trying to be consistent with his promises. He was demonstrating that he was, indeed, willing to give his life in defense of his Master. Good for Peter! It seems that he is about to show that Jesus was wrong in his previous assessments.

But strangely, Jesus does not defend himself and allows himself to be arrested. This baffles the disciples, especially Peter. They are willing to resort to violence, if necessary, but for Jesus to let himself be arrested and surrender to death's throes is just too much for the disciples. It seems that defending the Lord is one thing but following him in his death is another. How strange and unpredictable human nature is!

Then, all the disciples, including Peter, abandoned him and fled.

THE DAY OF BITTER WEEPING

While Peter was below in the courtyard, one of the servant girls of the high priest came by. When she saw Peter warming himself, she looked closely at him. "You also were with that Nazarene, Jesus," she said. But he denied it.

"I don't know or understand what you're talking about," he said, and went out into the entryway.

When the servant girl saw him there, she said again to those standing around, "This fellow is one of them." Again, he denied it.

After a little while, those standing near said to Peter, "Surely you are one of them, for you are a Galilean."

He began to call down curses, and he swore to them, "I don't know this man you're talking about." Immediately the rooster crowed the second time. Then Peter remembered the words Jesus had spoken to him: "Before the rooster crows twice you will disown me three times." And he broke down and wept (Mark 14:66–72).

At this point we reach the climax of human failure. We see Peter cry, and as Matthew and Luke say, "cry bitterly." I think this is the external sign of total and absolute failure. Anybody that has not experienced this type of crying probably has not "hit rock bottom" yet. That person still does not altogether despair of himself. Somewhere down deep inside, he still harbors some degree of self-confidence.

The story begins with Peter following from afar as Jesus is led before the high priest. Peter wants to be faithful to his Master and, although keeping a safe distance, he tries to stay close. Taking a risk, he enters the courtyard of the high priest's house and, trying to go unnoticed, joins a group of temple guards.

Suddenly Peter is discovered by one of the servant girls of the high priest: "You were with Jesus, the Nazarene." Peter denies it, saying, "I don't know him, and I don't know what you mean." Immediately he went out, trying to sneak away. Then a rooster crowed.

Once again, the servant girl sees him and accuses him, "This is one of them." But Peter again denies it. The third time, he is recognized by those who were at the entrance of the high priest's house. Then, Peter in his desperation to convince his adversaries, begins to curse[25] and swear, "I don't know the man you're talking about!"

At that very moment, the rooster crowed for the second time, and Peter remembered the words the Lord had spoken to him. According to Luke, what made Peter remember Jesus's words was that when the rooster crowed for the second time, Jesus, who was inside the house, turned and looked right at Peter. Can you imagine what that look meant for Peter? How must he have felt? Although it must have been a look of love, it surely disarmed him completely. Jesus's gaze was one of those piercing, penetrating looks that leaves you stripped and undone.

CONCLUSION

Thus, the eighteen discipleship lessons come to a dramatic close in the person of Peter. The process ends with a bitter cry that is nothing less than the expression of utter failure and deception.

We have seen that this journey of repeated failures and falls not only portrays Peter and his companions, but us as well. In our case, however, the situation is even more dramatic. Unlike the first disciples, the Holy Spirit dwells in us from the very day of our salvation.

In fact, the disciples could use the excuse that their failures were due to not having the Holy Spirit. But this excuse does not apply to those of us who live on this side of Pentecost. We enjoy the Spirit from the beginning of our call to follow Christ.[26] What, then, is the explanation for our helplessness in keeping the commandments of Jesus Christ? Their failure seems understandable, but not ours. In any case, don't despair or get discouraged because there is an explanation, as we will see later. First, however, let's go back to those first disciples' story to see how it ends.

According to Mark's gospel, the disciples, aware of their Master's death but not of his resurrection, are mourning and weeping (16:10). The risen Lord appeared to Mary Magdalene first, and then to two of them on their way to the country. But neither testimony is accepted nor believed by the other disciples, until finally, the Lord himself had to appear to the eleven to convince them of his resurrection.

According to John's gospel, Jesus appeared to his disciples alive on three separate occasions. Once when Thomas was not present, the second time when Thomas was present, and the third time when seven of them were fishing. One of those seven, apostle John, records an interesting fact in his gospel that can help us see how much the disciples had learned and how empty of themselves they had become.

John says that on that night when they went out fishing, they didn't catch anything. At dawn, Jesus appears on the shore and asks them, "Children, do you have any fish?"

"No", they answered.

Then Jesus tells them, "Cast the net on the right side of the boat, and you will find some."

Then something interesting happens. John says that, without question, without a doubt, and without an argument,[27] they cast the net and couldn't retrieve it because of the large quantity of fish. You are probably thinking, "Hallelujah!" because of the miracle, but I say "Hallelujah!" not for the miracle but for the disciples' plain, pure, and simple obedience. This obedience is simple and trusting like that of a child, something highly valued before God. Yet it has taken the Son of God no less than three and a half long years to forge it in his disciples.[28]

Now, if you still don't find it extraordinary that the disciples could show this kind of obedience, keep in mind that John warns that when the disciples obeyed the man who spoke to them from the beach, they didn't know it was Jesus (21:4). Hallelujah! What has taken place? The disciples are so broken, so void of any confidence in themselves, that they can obey "anyone" without constraint.

There is, however, a conversation pending between Jesus and Peter, which apostle John records in his gospel, that will show with absolute clarity the significant change that has occurred in the disciples.

After that breakfast on the beach, Jesus addressed Peter with the following question, "Simon, son of John, do you love me more than these?"

He replied, "Yes, Lord; you know that I love you." What is interesting is that when Jesus asks, "do you love me?" he is using the Greek verb *agape*. On the other hand, when Peter answers "I love you" he uses the Greek verb *phileo*.

Agapao Y Phileo

Agapao and *Phileo* are two Greek verbs that are both customarily translated as "love." From agapao, we get the noun *agape* in Greek that means "love." Phileo, meanwhile, comes from "philos," better translated as "friend." Both verbs, although often rendered as "love," are not synonymous. Even though agapao and phileo denote two different kinds of love, strictly speaking, only agapao should be translated as "love." In contrast, phileo should be translated as "care for" or "be fond of." In the New Testament, both verbs acquire particular connotations.

Indeed, the New Testament writers reserve the verb agapao mostly to refer to God's love, while phileo appears more in relation to human love. In this sense, it seems that the intention of the inspired writers of the New Testament was to establish that only the divine nature can express the verb agapao. On the other hand, the maximum expression of human nature is phileo love.

Let's take a closer look at this limitation of human nature, and why phileo should be translated as "care for," rather than "love." The life of apostle Peter is a perfect illustration of this situation. In the Gospel of John, Jesus Christ taught a tremendous maxim. He said, "Greater love (gr. agape) has no one than this, to lay down one's life for one's friends" (15:13). Two things emerge from this text: (1) agape love is the greatest love; (2) agape love has its maximum expression in the act of giving up one's life (lit. "laying down the soul"). The point is that Jesus Christ affirms four times in this gospel that he lays down his life (his soul) for his sheep (10:11, 15, 17, and 18). Therefore, he says, "I am the good shepherd," and "This is why the Father loves me."

Now, during the last night that Jesus spent with his disciples (John 13), he anticipated the moment of the cross by warning his disciples that they could not go where he was going. "And where are you going, Lord?" asked Simon Peter.

Jesus repeated, "Where I am going, you cannot follow me now, but you will follow me later."

In a sincere attempt to imitate his Master, Peter insists on the question, "Why can't I follow you now? I will give my life for you."

Jesus replies, "Will you give your life for me? Truly, truly, I say to you, the rooster won't crow until you have denied me three times."

Only a man who does not know himself would dare say, "I will give my life for you!" But since Jesus agreed that Peter could follow him later, he would first allow him to suffer the most significant setback of his life. For Peter, to one day be able to follow Christ to death, he would have to be broken. And indeed, before that night had ended, Peter had already denied his Lord. For Peter, all attempts to imitate his Master ended in bitter weeping (Mt. 26:75).

Therefore, when the resurrected Lord Jesus Christ met Peter again and had this new conversation with him, Peter did not dare answer his Master with the word agapao. Why? Peter has learned the lesson. He realizes that he doesn't have that greater love that would allow him to give his life for his friends. The Lord knows it, and now Peter knows it too.

The Lord asks him a second time, "Simon, son of John, do you love me?" Peter replied, "Yes, Lord; You know that I love you". Again, the Lord asks using "agapao" and, once again, Peter responds with "phileo." The Lord wants to make sure that Peter indeed has learned the lesson.

But what does Peter mean by answering with "phileo"? This word is sometimes translated as "to kiss" (Matthew 26:48, Mark 14:44, Luke 22:47). The verb phileo means to show affection. It means to care for someone. In effect, what Peter means to express with his answer is, "Yes, Lord, I desire to love you." "Yes, Lord, I want to love you." This is the maximum that human nature can offer. Agape love is exclusively the fruit of the Spirit.

But let's go back to the story. Jesus Christ asks him the third time, "Simon, son of John, do you love me?" Peter was grieved that Jesus would ask for the third time, "Do you love me?" At first glance, it seems that Peter's grief was due to the Lord's asking him the same thing three times. But that isn't the case. Peter's sorrow was because the third time the Lord used "phileo," not "agapao."

In other words, the cause of Peter's grief was because the Lord kept insisting. Paraphrasing, the Lord asked the third time, "Simon, son of John, in your own words, are you saying that you only care about me?" "Simon, son of John, should I understand from your words that you merely have affection for me?" Peter, saddened to be confronted with his flawed human reality, this time does not say yes but rather, "Lord, you know everything. You know that I care about you."

However, in the days following, Peter's life would change wonderfully. He would be filled with the Holy Spirit and God's "agape" love (cf. Romans 5:5). The Bible states that Peter loved the Lord Jesus Christ with all his being, and from secular history we learn that Peter did, indeed, give his life for his Lord. He died crucified. Amen.

1   Diccionario de la lengua española, 23.ª ed., [versión 23.3 en línea]. <https://dle. rae.es> 10 September 2020.
2   One is not possible without the other. Just knowing him, we get to know ourselves.
3   Cf Genesis 41.32
4   One denarii was generally equivalent to a day's wage for an unskilled worker.
5   Between three o'clock and six o'clock of the morning.
6   Literally, "Are you also that slow?"
7   In both cases (6.52 and 7.18) the Greek verb used is the same: suniemi.
8   Remember: 18 = 6 + 6 + 6.
9   In the context, the leaven of the Pharisees seems to be related to requiring signs without showing a believing attitude. According to Luke, the issue is hypocrisy (12.1) and according to Matthew, it is the teaching of the Pharisees (16.12).
10 The leaven of Herod seems to have been the use of political power against the believers.
11 "Satan" means enemy and adversary.
12 2 Timothy 2.12.
13 Matthew says that while Peter was still speaking, a cloud of light covered them all.
14 James 1.19.
15 Luke 9.51.
16 The verb "to be indignant" in Greek is aganakteo.
17 Matthew 19.28.
18 It is likely that James and John's mother (Salome) was the sister of Mary, Jesus's mother (Mark 15.40, Matthew 27.56, John 19.25).
19 The same verbal expression in Greek used by Mark in 10.14.
20 The New Century Version states in 14.27, "You will all stumble in your faith."
21 See Exodus 20.21, Deuteronomy 4.11, 1 Kings 8.12, 2 Chronicles 6.1.
22 Revelation 14.4.
23 A mixture of astonishment and horror according to the Interlineal New Testament.
24 A very annoying feeling, like being helplessly "outside of yourself." (Interlinear).
25 The Greek verb is anathematize. This comes from the word *anathema*.
26 Ephesians 1.13–14.
27 Compare Luke 5.5.
28 It is noteworthy that John states that the disciples have already received the Holy Spirit (20.22).

2

WAITING

When failure is total and complete, as was the case with Jesus's disciples, the effect is so shattering and absolute as to paralyze you and leave you with no strength to do anything. The disciples certainly felt that way. For this reason, the Lord appeared to them several times after his resurrection, to lift them out of their despair. His expression "peace be with you" had to be followed by incontrovertible proofs of their Master's resurrection, which would ultimately convince them in the end.

Then came the instruction from the Lord that we know as "the Great Commission," found in all four gospels. However, only Luke, the evangelist, points out that the instructions given by the Lord were not meant to be acted upon immediately. According to Luke, Jesus added a big "*but*" before they could get to work, "but stay in the city of Jerusalem, until ..." What is the reason for this "but"? "Behold," said Jesus, "I will send my Father's promise." According to Luke, the Father promised they would be empowered from above.[1]

Luke is even more explicit in his second book, Acts, which states that Jesus commanded them not to leave Jerusalem but to wait for the promise of the Father (1:4). Without the "promise of the Father," they were not to do anything. Thus, failure is followed by waiting. Otherwise, what would have been the sense of sending out the disciples on that great commission with nothing more than they already had, after all the failures they had experienced? The result would have been more of the same: increased failure. They needed the strength of *Another* if they were to go out and serve their Lord. And that additional strength would come from none other than the Holy Spirit. Therefore, they were not to leave Jerusalem until the Holy Spirit had come upon them. Only then would they be capable of being witnesses (martyrs) for Christ, not only in Jerusalem but also throughout Judea, Samaria, and to the ends of the Earth.

OUR SITUATION

At this point, it would be good to pause for a bit and evaluate our own situation. We said earlier that our condition is more dramatic than that of the disciples because we, contrary to them, have had the Holy Spirit from the beginning of our Christian life. So how do we explain our failure? Our Christian life does not include any stage without the Holy Spirit, as was the case with the disciples. So, if the disciples' failures were due to not having the Holy Spirit dwelling in them, how could the same failure be explained in our case? There is an explanation. Let's look.

Our big mistake has been to assume that, since we have the Holy Spirit right from the moment of our conversion, we are exempt from going through the experience of failure. Indeed, this mistake is unconscious; nonetheless, it is still a mistake. In our total ignorance and misunderstanding of our nature, we think that we should have no problem at all following the Lord once we receive the Holy Spirit. We thus ignore the fundamental fact that the interaction of the Holy Spirit is directly proportional to the decrease of the prominence of our own human nature. These cannot coexist. Either we are in control, or the blessed Holy Spirit is.

The most significant difference between the disciples and us is that at the time they received the Holy Spirit, they were utterly devoid of themselves due to the continuous series of failures. In our case, at the time when we were filled with the Spirit, we were also full of ourselves. So, parallel to the Spirit's filling, we had to gradually and progressively be emptied of ourselves. This is like having to fill a warehouse with boxes of a new product. It is one thing to do that with an empty room, and quite another if it is already full of other products. In the latter case, the warehouse can only be filled with the new product to the extent that it is emptied of the previous product.

As believers on this side of Pentecost, we have the blessed Holy Spirit from the moment of our salvation, but for the Spirit to take control of our lives, we need to be emptied of ourselves. And to the same degree that we move into second place, the Spirit can take control of us. In other words, what the disciples had to live in two separate stages, we experience simultaneously.

Our mistake was thinking that we could do things with the Holy Spirit's help, instead of recognizing that the Christian life is the Holy Spirit living through us. And so, once saved, we quickly attempt to show goodness through our own efforts, rather than allowing the new life we have received to reveal itself. Worst of all, in our attempt to please God—in a very real, albeit unconscious, competition with the Spirit—our humanity takes the place of the new life and relegates the new life to the background. Thus, even though we have the Holy Spirit, defeat sadly becomes our reality. So, if we are to be victorious one day, our humanity must necessarily be weakened, broken, and moved into second place.

More than action on our part, what is needed is surrender; more than effort, docility. In following Jesus, what matters most is not whether we have the Spirit, but how much the Spirit has of us. Because to the same extent that he has us, the Spirit has the freedom to dwell in or act through us. The Christian life is not about our helping God. We should indeed help each other, but God does not need our help. He is entirely sufficient in and of himself.

Neither does the Christian life consist of God helping us. Few people understand this point. Just as God is not interested in our help, neither is he interested in helping anyone, because that would mean that we are continuing to live and take the leading role in our lives. No, what the Lord is willing to do is take control of our lives and put us in second place. Of course, the Lord does not impose his will on us. He awaits our surrender.

Previously we ignored such fundamental truths as "it is no longer I who live, but it is Christ who lives in me."[2] "We who do not live according to the flesh, but according to the Spirit."[3] "We who serve God by his Spirit ... and who put no confidence in the flesh,"[4] etc.

Now we can understand something that always drew our attention. Why did the Holy Spirit's coming upon the disciples mean something vastly different from his coming upon us? It's as if they received a Spirit distinct from the one that we have received. We can now see that the difference was not in the glorious and blessed Holy Spirit but in us. The disciples were emptied of themselves at the time they were filled with the Spirit; we, on the other hand, were not. They were beaten down; we were still standing. Instead of being surrendered and docile, we have continuously competed with the Spirit. Given these circumstances, the most spiritual thing we could do was to allow the Spirit to help us. What a vain presumption!

Additionally, all of this was aggravated by a gospel that continuously impelled us to action. "You can do it: you have the Holy Spirit!" "Wanting is power!" "Go ahead, you are able!" "Strive!" "Fight!". This gospel has not only made our Christian life even more painful and frustrating, but it also considerably lengthened the process of brokenness. Instead of three and a half years, it could take thirty or forty years. Perhaps the saddest part is that many have been left lying along the roadside believing that, with failure upon failure, they just weren't up to the challenge.

But is there a biblical example we can point to that illustrates this painful but at the same time glorious experience? Of course! Let's consider apostle Paul's testimony in Romans 7.

PAUL'S TESTIMONY

> We know that the law is spiritual; but I am unspiritual, sold as a slave to sin. I do not understand what I do. For what I want to do I do not do, but what I hate I do. And if I do what I do not want to do, I agree that the law is good. As it is, it is no longer I myself who do it, but it is sin living in me. For I know that good itself does not dwell in me, that is, in my sinful nature. For I have the desire to do what is good, but I cannot carry it out. For I do not do the good I want to do, but the evil I do not want to do—this I keep on doing. Now if I do what I do not want to do, it is no longer I who do it, but it is sin living in me that does it. So I find this law at work: Although I want to do good, evil is right there with me. For in my inner being I

delight in God's law; but I see another law at work in me, waging war against the law of my mind and making me a prisoner of the law of sin at work within me. What a wretched man I am! Who will rescue me from this body that is subject to death? Thanks be to God, who delivers me through Jesus Christ our Lord! So then, I myself in my mind am a slave to God's law, but in my sinful nature a slave to the law of sin (7:14–25 NIV).

First, let us establish that Paul, like all believers on this side of Pentecost, had the Holy Spirit from the very moment of his salvation. Ananias stated this during his visit: "'Brother Saul, the Lord Jesus, who appeared to you on the road as you were coming here, has sent me so that you may see again and be filled with the Holy Spirit.' Immediately, something like scales fell from Saul's eyes, and he could see again. He got up and was baptized."[5]

If there is any doubt about it, consider Paul's own account of his conversion, where he states that Ananias asked him, "And now what are you waiting for? Get up, be baptized and wash your sins away, calling on his name."[6]

Second, consider the theological placement of chapter 7 within the epistle to the Romans. At a cursory glance, it seems that chapter 7 is misplaced. Indeed, chapter 6 of Romans is naturally and logically followed by chapter 8, not 7. But truth be told, chapter 7 is not misplaced. Paul wants to explicitly state that what happened in chapter 7 happened to him when he was already a Christian, not before. If what Paul said in chapter 7 were before chapter 6, we could probably infer that this happened to him when he was not a believer in Jesus Christ.

Even though, according to chapter 6, Paul knows that he has been justified and has received the objective revelation of the cross and deliverance from sin, nevertheless, in chapter 7 he experiences total and absolute failure. Sufficient testimony of that is found in the following expressions:

I do not understand what I do. For what I want to do I do not do, but what I hate I do. (7:15 NIV)

For I know that good itself does not dwell in me, that is, in my sinful nature. (7:18 NIV).

For I delight in the law of God according to the inner man, but I see another law in my members, warring against the law of my mind and bringing me into captivity to the law of sin which is in my members. O wretched man that I am! Who will deliver me from the body of this death? (MEV)

If this is not a total and absolute failure, then I don't know what it is! But what happened to Paul? The same thing that often happens to us! Failure came when, after being saved, he got up and wanted to please God. The problem is that he tried to do it in the power of his strength; in other words, in self-power.[7] This condition is what Paul calls "walking in the flesh." How do we know? According to chapter 8, Paul experienced victory when he learned to walk in the Spirit. Let us look at the precise statements in this regard:

There is therefore now no condemnation to those who are in Christ Jesus, who do not walk according to the flesh, but according to the Spirit. (8:1 New King James Version)

...that the righteous requirement of the law might be fulfilled in us who do not walk according to the flesh but according to the Spirit. (8:4 NKJV)

But you are not in the flesh but in the Spirit. (8:9 NKJV)

For as many as are led by the Spirit of God, these are sons of God. (8:14 NKJV)

Receiving the Spirit is a guarantee of salvation but not necessarily of victory unless we have learned to walk in the Spirit. Paul had enjoyed the abiding of the Spirit since his conversion, but until he encountered the experience of chapter 8, failure was the recurring experience. This is his testimony.

Like us, Paul thought that once he had received the Spirit, he could please his Lord. He did not yet understand that self had to be dethroned first if he were to do God's will. Only failure leads us to this experience and can, as a result, introduce us to the reality of the Spirit's power. Having the Spirit is one thing, but walking in the Spirit is another. The first says that we are saved; the second testifies that we are victorious. The Galatians had new life by grace and by the Spirit, yet they wanted to be perfected by the flesh. Paul tells them that this is a mistake:

> Are you so foolish? Although you began with the Spirit, are you now trying to finish by human effort? (3:3 New English Translation)

Not only justification is by faith but also sanctification. This is Pauline theology. Sanctification is also by faith. But what does it mean to say that sanctification is by faith? In the negative, it means that sanctification is not by works or by human effort. However, stated positively, it means that sanctification is through the Spirit. Faith is directly related to the person of the Holy Spirit. To declare, then, that sanctification is by faith means to declare that sanctification is by the Spirit.

According to Paul, "by faith" cannot only mean believing an objective truth and confessing it. No, that would not be enough without the reality of the Spirit. This is the case of the so-called "positive confession."

What then is Paul's solution for the Galatians?

> If we live in the Spirit, let us also walk in the Spirit. (5:25 NKJV)

"Walking in the Spirit" is Paul's answer to the problem of the Galatians. They had the Spirit, yet they did not walk in the Spirit. These are, as can be seen, two different experiences. Only the second makes us victorious because from the point of view of experience, says Paul, only by being led by the Spirit are we not under the law.[8]

OF WHAT DOES WAITING CONSIST?

When failure is total, the wait is natural and spontaneous. But how long will the waiting last? No one knows. All that Jesus has said is that "... in a few days" (NIV). In the case of the disciples, that wait lasted ten days. But in other cases, those "ten days" can and could mean several months, or even years. The point is that death that encompasses failure must necessarily be followed by a resurrection; that is, being lifted by the strength of "Another." Until that happens, there is nothing that can be done. Just wait.

But this waiting is not passivity, nor is it inactivity. Waiting has to do with hope, with having expectations. Therefore, Luke indicates that once they returned to the city of Jerusalem, they went to the upper room to await the Father's promise. The eleven apostles; the women; Mary, the mother of Jesus; and his brothers were gathered there.

All of these, according to Lucas, "persevered unanimously in prayer and supplication." And "When the Day of Pentecost had fully come, they were all with one accord in one place" (NKJV). This passage clearly spells out what "waiting" means:

CONTINUED9

Those who were assembled there did not know how long the wait would take, so they "continued" or "persevered." Perseverance is the first characteristic of a purely spiritual "waiting," and it is natural and spontaneous insofar as it is the fruit of total and complete failure. What else can be done when there is no strength left to do anything? Just wait and continue to wait, persevering in the wait. No matter how long it takes, whether ten days or a year, there is nothing to be done except wait. The Spanish Interlinear New Testament, instead of "persevere," translates this as "dedicate oneself steadfastly." This verb will also appear in Acts 2:42, 46; 6:4. It carries the idea of holding onto something bravely, forcefully, powerfully, intensely.

WITH ONE ACCORD10

"With one accord" means "with the same spirit." Other versions say, "in the same mind." It means "all of them with the same purpose." The Greek term *Omothumadon* also appears in Acts 2:46, 4:24, 5:12, and 15:25. This is the second characteristic of a spiritual wait. Perseverance is one thing, but persevering with one accord is another. From the texts mentioned here, it can be seen that these two characteristics remained in the disciples over time. This became their lifestyle, and it couldn't be any other way; these characteristics were forged into the disciples during the wait.

TOGETHER

"Together" indicates that the wait did not take place individually but collectively and corporately. The reason is quite simple: A collective effort produces synergy. So, it is one thing to try to persevere alone and quite another to persevere together. Individually we will not hang on long enough; together, however, we will. This third characteristic would also become a permanent life principle among the disciples and the early converts (2:44, 46; 3:1).

IN PRAYER AND SUPPLICATION

Thus, we come to the fourth and final characteristic of waiting—the most important of them. "Together" and "steadfastly dedicated" is the way scripture describes how the disciples of the Lord awaited the coming of the Holy Spirit. But the question is together and steadfastly dedicated to what? To prayer! Waiting for the powerful intervention of the Holy Spirit is done in prayer and supplication. The three characteristics previously stated are in relation to, and are a result of, prayer.

They persevered ("continued steadfastly") in prayer; they were of one accord in prayer, and they were praying together. They persevered together, of one accord, in prayer and supplication before the Lord. This is waiting.

Therefore, absolute failure must necessarily lead us finally to prayer. If this is not the case, or if prayer does not arise as a necessity, it would mean unequivocally that our failure is not yet total and complete. Let's say it again, with all its implications and with all honesty: If the failures in our Christian life do not lead us to the urgent need for prayer and supplication, it's because we have not yet "hit rock bottom." Any result other than prayer will be an indicator that our failure process has not yet terminated. Until then, everything will be partial.

The extent of my failure determines the level of prayer in my Christian life and, consequently, the degree of freedom that the Holy Spirit will have to act without opposition or resistance on my part. Ultimately, the degree of failure will thus be directly proportional to the degree of victory that I will eventually experience.

But why is prayer so important? Because it is through prayer that we manifest our dependence on the Lord Jesus Christ! The Christian life is like having to walk on the waters of the sea. Since this is impossible for us humanly, just as it was for Peter, we need a word from the Lord that allows us, enables us, and directs us to go to him on the waters. But not only that. We also need to keep our eyes on Jesus permanently. Otherwise, like Peter, we will begin to sink.

Waiting, then, is a stage and a principle of life. In their waiting, as a stage of Christian life, the disciples persevered in prayer and supplication for ten days. However, they later made prayer something that was constant and continuous.[11] This is what we mean when we say that waiting was a stage in the disciples' lives, as well as a life principle.

In these days, at the precise time that I was writing these pages—and because of those "coincidences" of the Lord—a book came into my hands that speaks precisely of the need to make the characteristics of waiting a principle of life. In it, the author says, "I often find people who tell me they just don't understand their situation. They explain to me that some years ago they reached the point of renouncing all attempts to save themselves by their own means or effort, and that they did indeed find victory. And I don't doubt that. I am sure that several years ago they really did reach the limit of themselves. They 'hit rock bottom.' The problem is that they are no longer 'hitting rock bottom' at the time they talk to me."[12]

Do you understand? If one's dependence on the Lord and his Spirit is not permanent, neither will victory be permanent. If "waiting" is only one stage in your life, you will stop trusting in the Lord once you achieve victory, and sooner rather than later, you will know defeat again.

In other words, we are all like Maradona, the famous Argentinean soccer player: Chronically ill, we can never be "discharged." We will never, ever be free from the "dependency" on sin. For this reason, we must never, ever release ourselves from dependence on the Lord! Only by remaining dependent on him will we be permanently victorious.

The ultimate reason for this is simply that the Lord is more interested in conquering us than in making us victorious. He wants to make us his, forever. Therefore, he designed everything so that, one way or another, all things will eventually lead us to him. Everything outside of him proves transitory so that we finally return to God. If we are more interested in his things than we are in him, the Lord will not allow himself to be used or manipulated. He might give us his things for a time, but without him, those things will never really be ours. The Lord wants to make us permanently dependent on him to make us his eternally. Hallelujah!

So then, this permanent dependence on our Master is made practical and real through prayer. In other words, if failure does not lead us to Christ, taking us steadfastly to him, then it means that we have not yet diminished enough.

According to Paul, the divine pedagogy used by God in the Old Testament perfectly illustrates this point. Let's look.

DIVINE PEDAGOGY

According to Paul, God granted Abraham and his descendants the inheritance through the promise, not through the law that came 430 years later. The question is then, why did he give them the law? If the law could not give life, as Paul says, then what could be the meaning of giving it to Israel? God had a surprising purpose. Having determined to grant his righteousness through faith, he added the law at a point in Israel's history for the precise purpose of preparing God's people for faith.

How is that? God always knew that his righteousness could only be received as a gift—as a present. But man didn't know that. God also knew that humans, by their nature, would try to deserve it or make of it a personal achievement, instead of accepting it by faith. So how could Israel be prepared for faith? Through the law, which precisely stated: "The man who does those things shall live by them" (NKJV).

In other words, God gave them the law so that the people of Israel would discover that they could not keep the law, despite their best and most sincere attempts. Therefore, they would understand that the only way to righteousness was through faith, not through the works of the law. Ultimately, God gave them the law for approximately fifteen hundred years so that they would fail in their attempt to deserve God's righteousness.

Paul masterfully says it this way: "Therefore the law was our tutor to bring us to Christ" (NKJV). The law, like a good teacher, taught us that we were sinners and that we needed a Savior. Thus, it led us to Christ. Do you see that? Failure to keep the law brought Israel to Christ. This is the point we have been making all along: true failure necessarily leads us to Christ. Then, in him, through him and under him, we will experience a new life.

Being under the law is the attempt—failed, obviously—to please God using our own strength, and the result that God expects is that we be emptied of ourselves in our spirit. Only in this way does the blessedness promised to the "poor in spirit" reach us.

THE POOR IN SPIRIT

> Blessed are the poor in spirit, for theirs is the kingdom of heaven. (NIV)

Poverty, in general, implies "lacking," which could be either material or spiritual. Luke only speaks of the poor, while Matthew speaks about the poor in spirit. Each one approaches the issue of poverty from a different angle. Luke refers to material poverty and Matthew to spiritual poverty.

Indeed, Luke speaks not only of the poor but also of the hungry and the weeping—without qualifying them. However, in Matthew, these conditions are spiritualized: the poor are poor in spirit, and those who are hungry are hungry and thirsty for righteousness. The fact that Luke is referring to material poverty is confirmed, finally, by the four woes he adds to the beatitudes, which are the exact opposites of the blessings: "Woe to you who are rich! Woe to you who are well fed now! Woe to you who laugh now!" Therefore, in Luke, Jesus is addressing material poverty. How good it is that Jesus is not indifferent to material poverty! He brought the good news of the gospel to them as well.

On the other hand, in Matthew, Jesus speaks to spiritual poverty. Here the beatitudes are not only spiritualized but also presented as virtues—as positive qualities. Blessed are the peacemakers, the pure in heart, the merciful, the meek, those who hunger and thirst, the righteous. In Luke, they are deficiencies; in Matthew, they are virtues. In Luke, they are negative deficiencies; in Matthew, they are favorable qualities.

So, how should we interpret the first two beatitudes of Matthew? "Blessed are the poor in spirit and blessed are those who mourn." From the context, we infer that the mourning to which Matthew refers is different from the weeping mentioned by Luke. In Matthew, "mourning" is also a virtue; in Luke, on the other hand, the weeping he refers to is produced by suffering. Keeping to this line of thought, spiritual poverty is not a defect, but a Christian virtue.

In conclusion, Luke describes the state in which Jesus finds the world when he introduces the gospel, while on the other hand, Matthew describes the Christian character of those in whom the gospel has already operated. Spiritual poverty in Matthew is not, then, the condition in which God finds the lost sinner, but a quality that must be shown by the disciples of Christ, and possessing it is a reason for happiness.

What, then, is this virtue? To answer that question, we will look at the person who was most exceedingly poor in spirit. I refer to our Lord Jesus Christ. But first, let's ask ourselves: what inspired the Lord to highlight this fundamental beatitude by placing it first on the list? Obviously, that came from the Old Testament word of God, which he knew perfectly well. It was very likely the prophet Isaiah's words that inspired Jesus to declare, "Blessed are the poor in spirit." Let's look at Isaiah 57:15, where God says:

> I dwell in the high and holy place, with him also that is of a contrite and humble spirit, to revive the spirit of the humble, and to revive the heart of the contrite ones. (American King James Version)

How amazing! The High and Sublime dwells on high and in holiness. This is rightly so and is inherent to him. However, what is amazing is that God also lives with the broken and humble in spirit even in his greatness and holiness. God does not dwell with the proud—with the self-sufficient. He looks at the arrogant man only from afar. But God himself visits the contrite and humble in spirit, to quicken his spirit and make alive his heart. As Jesus said, "theirs is the kingdom of heaven."

Jesus Christ perfectly embodied this virtue, which is the first of the beatitudes and the fundamental key for evidencing the others. In the days of his flesh, Jesus declared:

> Most assuredly, I say to you, the Son can do nothing of Himself. (John 5:19 NKJV)

This passage shows what it means to be humble and poor in spirit. It is total distrust in our own limited resources, which leads us to do nothing without God. Jesus, who was not at all deceived by sin, knew better than anyone that the life he brought into the world could not be lived in the flesh's strength. Not even Jesus was exempt from that fact. Unlike us, he did not need a tutor to bring him to the knowledge of this truth, because he was never deceived by sin. The poor in spirit, then, know the impotence of their flesh, its corruption, and its malignancy.[13] So, like Christ, they have made a radical decision (i.e., do nothing for themselves).

In the case of Jesus Christ, this decision was absolute and accompanied him throughout his entire earthly life. In our case, unfortunately, it is relative and partial. If Jesus's decision had not had those characteristics, surely, he too would have sinned and would have become one more fallen being. But since he was aware of this truth, our blessed Lord always lived connected to his Father through the Holy Spirit and never did anything on his own.

Later, Paul would say it like this:

> For you know the grace of our Lord Jesus Christ, that though He was rich, yet for your sake He became poor, that you through His poverty might become rich. (2 Corinthians 8:9)

"Though he was rich, he became poor." To what type of poverty does this refer? Material or spiritual poverty? Many have wanted to see here a reference to the material poverty of Jesus. However, I consider it relatively unimportant to discuss this point. The text is quite clear regarding the initial question that we have asked ourselves. The text says that Jesus became poor so that with his poverty, we would be enriched. You see, he enriched us with his poverty.

Therefore, Paul cannot be referring to the material poverty of Jesus but rather to his spiritual poverty. He enriched us with his spiritual poverty. In his divine capacity (being rich), he could have done all things for himself and did not need to depend on anything or anyone. He is God. However, Jesus, as a man, became poor and did nothing on his own, so that the rest of us would be enriched by his spiritual secret and learn from his example to live the Christian life as he lived it.

We must always remember that this is the only possible way to live the Christian life. Therefore, the poor in spirit are blessed, for theirs is the kingdom of heaven. In other words, without resistance or opposition, the poor in spirit will show in themselves and through themselves the authority, power, and governance of God.

That is why we also said that this beatitude is not only the first but also the fundamental, or key, beatitude needed for evidencing the other beatitudes. Indeed, only the poor in spirit weep. We have already said that this weeping is not the fruit of suffering but rather of spiritual poverty. It is an expression of our dependence on the Lord. Hence, Luke says that the disciples "continued" in prayer and supplication.

In the same way, only the poor in spirit are meek. Because they are not self-confident, they can easily work with others and form a team. When you do things for yourself, you will inevitably fall into others' contempt, just as the Pharisees did (Luke 18:9).

Only the poor in spirit hunger and thirst for righteousness. Since they have no righteousness of their own, they are hungry and thirsty for it. They also know that this righteousness can only come from heaven. As Paul said, I want "to be found in Him, not having my own righteousness, which is from the law, but that which is through faith in Christ, the righteousness which is from God by faith" (NKJV).

The poor in spirit are also merciful. They know that they are no better than anyone else.

Their status as poor in spirit makes them pure in heart and so on.

Therefore, we could paraphrase the beatitudes in light of their meaning, as follows:

"Blessed are those who have learned not to do anything apart from Christ because in them the power of God will be manifest.

Blessed are those who show their dependence on the Lord with tears because they will be comforted by the powerful support of God's power.

Blessed are those who work as a team because they know that they cannot do it alone, for theirs is the land of victory.

Blessed are those who hunger and thirst for the righteousness of Christ since they have no righteousness of their own, because they will be clothed with it.

Blessed are those who recognize that they are no better than anyone else and, therefore, treat others with the same mercy with which they were treated.

Blessed are those who, through faith, have a heart clothed in the purity of Christ, because it allows them to contemplate God.

Blessed are those who have nothing of their own to defend, thus contributing to peace because they will be recognized as God's true children.

Blessed are those who are looked down upon by those who have their own righteousness, because the righteousness of the kingdom justifies them."

Amen.

1   Luke 24:49.

2   Galatians 2:20.

3   Romans 8:4.

4   Philippians 3:3.

5   Acts 9:17–18.

6   Acts 22:16.

7   Eight times Paul uses some form of pronoun first person singular, "I", in Romans 7:7–25.

8   Galatians 5:18.

9   Greek *proskartereo*. Translator's note: Many Spanish translations of this scripture use the word "persevere" in Acts 1:14, but none of the common English translations use that exact word, although they imply it. Most English translations use the word "continued," or phrases like "joined together constantly," "constantly devoting themselves." However, the concept that the author highlights here is the perseverance of the disciples. Also, many English translations do not have "… and supplication", which the author specifically references. The translation that best transmits both concepts here is the New King James Version (NKJV), which we have used here: "…these all continued with one accord in prayer and supplication, with the women and Mary the mother of Jesus, and with His brothers."

10   Greek *Omothumadon*.

11   See Acts 6:4, Romans 12:12, Ephesians 6:18, Colossians 4:2. In each case the verb "proskartereo" of Acts 1:14 appears.

12   Wells Michael, "Lost in the Desert," 168.

13   Behind the flesh is the self constantly seeking glory.

3

VICTORY

After the defeat comes the wait; after the wait comes the victory. This was the third phase in the life of the disciples and is where most books on Christian discipleship begin. However, it is not possible to understand clearly what this last phase meant in the life of the disciples without considering the two previous ones. This is especially true when we want to understand the marvelous and extraordinary effects—radically different from our own experience—that Pentecost had on these men.

The third and last phase began at Pentecost with the glorious and blessed coming of the Holy Spirit. Following three and a half years of failure in their attempt to measure up to the standard of their Master and, following that, waiting another ten days, united in prayer and supplication, the day of Pentecost finally arrived.

> When the day of Pentecost had come, they were all together in one place.

> And suddenly there came from heaven a noise like a violent rushing wind, and it filled the whole house where they were sitting. And there appeared to them tongues as of fire distributing themselves, and they rested on each one of them.

> And they were all filled with the Holy Spirit and began
> to speak with other tongues, as the Spirit was giving them
> utterance. (Acts 2:1–4)

Just as the Lord Jesus had promised them when he said, referring to the Spirit of truth, "You will know him because he abides with you, and will be in you," the disciples were now full of the Holy Spirit.

The great difference with us who are on this side of Pentecost is that, thanks to the two previous stages, the Holy Spirit found the disciples empty of themselves and completely open to his action in their lives. For this reason, we dare call this phase "The Victory."

With the coming and the filling of the Holy Spirit, the disciples began to live, not in their own strength, but through the life of the other who now lives in them. Only in this way does the impossible become possible for the disciples. In this sense, it is striking and does not cease to surprise us that although Jesus Christ has carried out a complete and perfect work and has overcome death forever by being raised from the dead, nevertheless, none of this can take place in the life of the disciples without the Holy Spirit. Therefore, it is impossible to overemphasize the importance of the glorious person of the Holy Spirit.

In any case, we must remember that we are speaking of victory, not so much with reference to the indwelling of the Spirit, but to the glorious fact that the disciples began to walk in the Spirit.

ACTS OR ACTIONS THAT MEASURE UP TO THE MASTER'S STANDARD

The book of Acts is the second treatise written by Luke, following his gospel that bears his name. Several purposes can be mentioned when determining the rationale behind this narrative. However, among the various objectives of the book, the following can be mentioned as among the most profound. Luke, inspired by the Holy Spirit, now records "the acts" of the disciples, and no longer the "acts" of Christ. What is extraordinary, however, is that the "acts" of the disciples for the first time measure up to the acts of their Master.

What takes place is that the Lord Jesus Christ, through the Holy Spirit, is being reproduced in the lives of the disciples. Everything that we see the Son of God living out in the Gospel of Luke is now reproduced in his church. The same "acts" of the gospel we will see here, however, no longer manifested in Christ, but rather in his church.

Paul, writing to the Philippians, explained that for him there was no greater objective than to become like Christ ...

> that I may know Him and the power of His resurrection and the fellowship of His sufferings, being conformed to His death; in order that I may attain to the resurrection from the dead. Not that I have already obtained it or have already become perfect, but I press on so that I may lay hold of that for which also I was laid hold of by Christ Jesus." (Philippians 3:10–12).

Now, this is precisely what we will see presented in the book of Acts. We will see here the "other" Christ—his church—doing and teaching the same as their Lord. Or better stated, we will see the Body of Christ manifested. Thus, we will observe the twelve disciples living in a new dimension, but not only the twelve. The rest of the disciples will also live at the level of their Savior. One will be like Christ in death, and another will follow the way of the cross in a manner like the Son of God.

Until chapter 6 of the book of Acts, the twelve apostles will be the main human protagonists, while the other disciples go through the typical process of post-Pentecost believers.[1] That is to say, the other disciples are learning and experiencing the difference between "receiving the Spirit" and "walking in the Spirit."

Later, after chapter 6 of Acts, we will see other disciples like Stephen and especially apostle Paul being raised by the Holy Spirit. They are not the only ones who measure up to their Master's standards; rather they are just a small sampling.

THE TWELVE

As soon as the twelve were filled with the Spirit, Peter got up to explain to the assembled crowd what had just happened. At least three things indicated that the one standing before them was not the same Peter as before, the impetuous one.

First, Peter, for the first time, is filled with the Spirit. Second, Peter does not act this time in his capacity as a disciple but as an apostle. Indeed, the same day that the church of our Lord Jesus Christ was born by the work and grace of the Holy Spirit, on that same day, the same Spirit manifested the twelve to be apostles. The manifestation of the church coincided with the manifestation of the first apostles, the twelve. Proof of this is found in the preaching of Peter that resulted in the conversion and baptism of about three thousand people.

Third, it is not an insignificant fact that Luke says that Peter, "standing up with the eleven, raised his voice …" The phrase "with the eleven" has great spiritual significance. It indicates that Peter is not acting on his own or in an individualistic manner. No, Peter is now acting in a corporate manner. He no longer rushes ahead or goes forth to act on his own but acts within the consensus of the body of Christ. Ultimately, although it is Peter who speaks, this time he does so on behalf of the twelve and not himself. Hallelujah!

Luke, with inspired precision, will continually allude to this change in attitude, not only of Peter but also of the other apostles: "And they continued steadfastly in the apostles' doctrine" (Acts 2:42).

It is not the doctrine of Peter but the doctrine of the apostles: "And fear came to every person; and many wonders and signs were done by the apostles" (Acts 2:43).

We do not know if each of the apostles did wonders and signs. Probably not, but to tell the truth, it doesn't matter, because they no longer are acting independently. Luke records that the many wonders were done by the apostles as a body.

> Now Peter and John were going up to the temple at the
> ninth hour, the hour of prayer. (Acts 3:1)

But Peter, along with John, fixed his gaze on him and said, "Look at us!" (Acts 3:4)

While he was clinging to Peter and John, all the people ran together to them at the so-called portico of Solomon, full of amazement. But when Peter saw this, he replied to the people, "Men of Israel, why are you amazed at this, or why do you gaze at us, as if by our own power or piety we had made him walk?" (Acts 3:11–12)

Now as they observed the confidence of Peter and John. (Acts 4:13)

But Peter and John answered and said to them... (Acts 4:19)

Had you been in Peter's place, would you have said: "Look at us?" Or, knowing that you were the person used to perform the miracle, would you have said like Peter, "Why do you gaze at us, as if by our own power or piety we had made him walk?

And with great power the apostles were giving testimony to the resurrection of the Lord Jesus, and abundant grace was upon them all. (Acts 4:33)

Bring the proceeds of the sales and lay them at the apostles' feet. (Acts 4:34–35)

At the hands of the apostles many signs and wonders were taking place among the people; and they were all with one accord in Solomon's portico. (Acts 5:12)

They laid hands on the apostles and put them in a public jail. (Acts 5:18)

But Peter and the apostles answered, "We must obey God rather than men." (Acts 5:29).

They took his advice; and after calling the apostles in, they flogged them and ordered them not to speak in the name of Jesus, and then released them. So they went on their way from the presence of the Council, rejoicing that they had been considered worthy to suffer shame for His name. And every day, in the temple and from house to house, they kept right on teaching and preaching Jesus as the Christ. (Acts 5:40–42)

So the twelve summoned the congregation of the disciples and said, "It is not desirable for us to neglect the word of God in order to serve tables." (Acts 6:2)

And these they brought before the apostles; and after praying, they laid their hands on them. (Acts 6:6)

What glory these texts reveal! There are no outstanding personalities or leading roles—no names nor hierarchies. Gone are the days of contending about who will be the greatest—the days of requests, privileges, and concessions. When we proceed like this, concerted and collectively as they did, only the name of Jesus is exalted and glorified. The corporate manifestation of the church allows for only the primacy of Christ to be seen over it.

ONE SIMILAR TO CHRIST IN HIS DEATH

In chapters 6–8 of the book of Acts, the writer Luke presents the life testimony of two individuals unknown until now: Stephen and Philip. What is Luke's intention? Luke intends to present us with two examples of what the Holy Spirit was able to do, not only with the apostles, but also with the post-Pentecost believers. We recall that up to chapter 6 of Acts, about three and a half years of church history had passed. Esteban and Felipe were probably present on the day the Holy Spirit appeared. But now, three and a half years after Pentecost, the Spirit raised up and revealed other men of apostolic stature.

This is even more significant if we consider that Stephen and Philip, up to the sixth chapter of Acts, appear as simple brothers. In modern language, they were not part of the "clergy"; they were simple "laity." Although in Acts chapter six both brothers become part of the team that is in charge of the work of "serving tables," nevertheless, the spiritual characteristics they possess at the time of their designation are impressive: (1) of good testimony, (2) filled with the Holy Spirit, and (3) full of wisdom. Concerning Stephen, who is the first of the seven to be mentioned, it is also added that he was a man full of faith. All these qualities are outstanding. Each one is an invitation to worship the Lord for his precious and powerful work of transformation. However, the best is yet to come.

Acts 6:7 declares that because of the congregational restructuring produced by the appointment of "the seven," not only were the expressed needs met, but special mention is made that "the word of the Lord grew." This expression does not refer to the increase in the number of the disciples, but to the fact that the word increased in their lives. The word, which is Christ himself, continued to become incarnate in the disciples. An outstanding example of this glorious fact is Stephen, who is the center of attention of biblical inspiration from 6:8 to the end of chapter 7.

Indeed, to those characteristics already mentioned, the following are now added: (1) full of grace, (2) full of power, and (3) he performed great wonders and signs among the people. None of this is of little importance. Stephen is the first to be mentioned doing miracles apart from the apostles. He was surely a much loved and duly recognized man in the church— young, outstanding and with a promising apostolic ministry. Having such a man in the church was undoubtedly a motive for great pride.

Only the Lord Jesus Christ, after much toil, had managed to form men of this stature: The twelve. Now, however, the Holy Spirit, through the life of the church, also raises up men who will be envoys or apostles. These are the works of Christ being reproduced by the Holy Spirit. However, for Stephen, the Lord has a more excellent way.

Unexpectedly and surprisingly for us, persecution arises against Stephen and from that moment in the life of our brother, an all too familiar scene begins to repeat itself: Jesus's arrest.[2] Indeed, as in the case of Jesus,[3] the opponents could not resist the wisdom and the Spirit with which Stephen spoke (6:10).

Second, as in the case of Jesus, Stephen's enemies stirred up the people and arrested him and brought him to the council (6:12).[4]

A third similarity between the arrest of Stephen and the arrest of Jesus is found in the fact that in both cases the opponents presented false witnesses to the council (6:13).[5] Furthermore, in both cases, the accusations were related to speaking blasphemous words against the temple (6:13–14; compare with Matthew 26:60–61; Mark 14:57–58). Up to here four amazing similarities between Jesus and Stephen. But the best is yet to come.

Then Luke records in chapter 7 of the book of Acts the speech that Stephen gave in his defense before the council. The reason was to make known the clear, powerful, and comprehensive revelation that God had given Stephen regarding his purpose. Herein is a very surprising fact. There is no record up to that point that the vision Stephen saw had ever been seen by anyone else, not even the twelve apostles. I personally have the conviction that Stephen was the first "Paul" the Lord raised up.

Now then, Stephen in his speech presented the following divine facts:

First, starting from the patriarch Abraham, Stephen established that the God of glory appeared to Abraham when he was in Mesopotamia and not when he was in the land of the Jews (7:1–8). Second, when God later revealed himself to Joseph, he was not in Canaan, but in Egypt (7:9–19). Third, Moses, after being rejected by his own brothers, fled to the land of Midian where he lived as a foreigner for forty years. He was here, and not in the land of the Israelites, when God appeared to him in the fire-engulfed bush (7:20–43). Fourth, our parents, Stephen says, had the tabernacle of testimony while in the desert and later brought it with Joshua to the promised land. Once established in the promised land, David wanted to provide a tabernacle for the God of Jacob (7:44–46). Fifth, although it was Solomon who finally built a house for the God of Jacob, Stephen masterfully clarifies, nevertheless, that the Most High does not dwell in temples made by hand, as the prophet says:

> "Heaven is my throne, and earth is the footstool of my feet; what kind of house will you build for me?" says the Lord, "Or what place is there for my repose? Was it not my hand which made all these things?" (Acts 7:49-50)

In an extraordinary way, then, Stephen reveals that our God cannot be restricted to one place, temple, race, or any culture. God transcends all human conditions and limits. He is the God of all men, of all nations, and of all lands. Nationalism and cultural identities, in general, are human reductionisms that limit men but not God. Now we can understand a little the anger and hatred that the Jews felt when listening to Stephen. Not only had he shattered the national pride of the Jewish race, but even worse, he had relativized the Jewish temple. The latter was what produced his death sentence.

Finally, Stephen's contemporaries—following the tradition of their fathers, who had rejected Joseph, Moses, and the prophets—were now traitors and murderers of the Just One. While the reaction of the people led these men to literally gnash their teeth in anger and hatred against him, Stephen, filled with the Holy Spirit, saw the glory of God and Jesus who was at the right hand of God. But when Stephen verbalizes what he is seeing, the listeners have a reaction that resembles the one they had experienced not that long ago, when Jesus himself had declared, "But from now on the Son of Man will sit at the right hand of the power of God (7:57, compared with Matthew 26:64–68)." This is a fifth similarity between the trial of Jesus and the trial of Stephen.

The sixth similarity, which is more glorious than the previous ones, takes place while Stephen is being stoned. During the stoning he invokes his Lord, with the same words that his Master had prayed to his Father. While hanging on the cross, Jesus had said: "Father, into your hands I commend my spirit" (Luke 23:46). Now Stephen, shortly before dying, says: "Lord Jesus, receive my spirit" (7:59).

At this point it is interesting to observe something that is not evident in the traditional Reina Valera Spanish version of the Bible, which is like the King James Version of the English Bible, but that is found in the Greek text, as well as in other modern versions. When Stephen sees the glory of God and Jesus who is at the right hand of God, the original text states that Jesus is standing at the right hand of God. All the other New Testament texts that refer to Jesus's position at the right hand of the Father say that Jesus is sitting, not standing. This is the only place in the entire New Testament where Jesus is said to be standing at the right hand of God. This fact, which is unique and unprecedented in the biblical record, must therefore have a very deep spiritual significance. And it does, although perhaps for now we can only guess as to what it is.

Jesus probably stands up to expectantly receive his disciple who is about to give his life for his Lord. Let us remember that Stephen had the privilege of being the first martyr of the Christian era. So perhaps heaven itself was silent and contemplated with respect and admiration such a great event.

I would dare to say something else. Perhaps, more than out of respect and admiration, Jesus stood up because he felt full of satisfaction that not only is someone dying for him, which is saying a lot, but because this someone is dying in a similar manner. Jesus contemplates in Stephen's death part of his own death. In some aspect he sees his death reproduced in Stephen's death. And this introduces us to the seventh and last similarity between the death of Christ and the death of Stephen.

In this seventh likeness, Stephen's death reaches its climax, and our brother shines and radiates with a glory like that of Christ himself. Indeed, in the process of stoning, Esteban, kneeling, cried out with a loud voice: "Lord, do not take this sin into account." And having said this, he slept (7:60). Only one person had previously expressed something similar: our blessed Lord Jesus Christ, when he suffered the cross of Calvary. There he had said: "Father, forgive them, for they do not know what they are doing" (Luke 23:34).

Now, someone filled with the spirit of Christ, Stephen, releases forgiveness on his enemies, saying, "Lord, do not hold this sin against them" (7:60).

Hallelujah! How glorious! Stephen thus achieved similarity to the Master in his death. Can you grasp the dimension of this fact? Pronouncing forgiveness is not easy, especially if we are talking about expressing forgiveness at the very moment that the offense is being received. But, in Stephen's case, we are talking about forgiving at the very moment that your enemies, like wild bulls, snort out their hatred and are stoning you to death. This is humanly impossible. Only someone like Jesus Christ can act like this—only he and those in whom his spirit and character are replicated by the mighty Holy Spirit. Well, in Stephen we have a beautiful example of this very thing.

For a long time, I have wondered why the Lord set Stephen on this pathway. Wouldn't it have been more profitable for God's plan to deliver Stephen from death, as he did later in the case of apostle Peter, for example? As I said earlier, wouldn't it have been better to allow "the first Paul" to develop his ministry, which was so promising? What blessing and fruit he would have brought to the Lord's work! With all certainty he would have been most useful in the Lord's plans.

To answer these questions, it is necessary to first answer another question, which gets to the bottom of the issue: What is the ultimate reason for our salvation and calling? What is it that conclusively explains the creation of man and the very development of our ministry? In short, are we here to be happy, to successfully develop a ministry, plant churches, travel the world evangelizing, preach, etc.? I hope not to surprise you, but the ultimate meaning of our life is none of these things.

What is it then? Paul states it clearly in his letter to the Romans:

> For those whom He foreknew, He also predestined to become conformed to the image of His Son, so that He would be the firstborn among many brethren. (Romans 8:29).

There is only one final destiny that God has for all his children (i.e., to be conformed to the image of his Son). Do you see what I mean? He is the image of God. That is why when God said, "Let us make man in our image" he was really saying, "Let us make man after the pattern of Christ." When we are made in the image of the Son, then we are made in the image of God. Is that clear? Therefore, everything exists for and is in accordance with this supreme purpose of God. Creation itself, redemption, gifts, ministries, marriage, children, and everything else find their ultimate cause in this pre-destiny of God.

So why didn't the Lord deliver Stephen? Because nothing is greater than attaining the image of Christ. Nothing is above this. And it fell to our beloved Stephen to be Christlike in perhaps the most difficult aspect of all, to be Christlike in his death.[6] Others, depending on the level of grace received, will probably show similarity to Christ in other circumstances (i.e., in their role as husband, son, wife, apostle, pastor, boss, slave, etc.).[7] The image of Christ has to do especially with character. This, once forged in us, manifests itself in every circumstance of life that we face. Stephen had to die in a manner like his Lord. He had the privilege of manifesting the character of Christ in that circumstance. It was something worth standing up for, right? Some the Lord can deliver, but with others, he follows a more excellent way.

To finish, there is an interesting point concerning Stephen. His name means "crown" and, coincidentally, in the seventh chapter of Acts an important stage of the church is "crowned." Indeed, from chapter 8 on, the church in Jerusalem will enter a new stage in its history. Until chapter 7, the church had been circumscribed only within the Jerusalem city limits, even though the Lord had sent them to the ends of the earth. Now, however, due to the persecution that began first against Stephen and then finally raged against the whole group, the church left the city surroundings and was "planted" in all Israel, and even beyond the national boundaries.

Therefore, we can say that until the seventh chapter of Acts, the church was a seed that was being prepared for sowing. But once the seed was ready, as seen in chapter 8, it begins to be "scattered" throughout Israel. What proves, however, that the seed was indeed mature? Precisely Stephen's death. With his death, the church's maturity process in Jerusalem is "crowned," and in heaven the go-ahead is given to start sowing.

With the death of Stephen, the warning given by our Lord Jesus Christ was physically and literally embodied, when he said: "Truly, truly, I say to you, unless a grain of wheat falls into the earth and dies, it remains alone; but if it dies, it bears much fruit" (John 12:24).

According to some historians, between one hundred and two hundred new churches were planted throughout Israel. From a single church, which existed in Jerusalem, the number grew to one hundred or more churches in a short period of time. And just as amazing, or even more so, is the fact that all these new churches were not planted by the apostles, but by the brothers themselves. Incredible!

It turned out to be true that if the seed dies, it bears much fruit.

But was Stephen a unique case? Was not the quality of his spiritual life an exception? We suspect not. Stephen might be the most prominent example, but by no means the only one.

Indeed, in the eighth chapter of the book of Acts, the main human character would now be Philip. Here testimony will be given of the outstanding spiritual stature of this brother, just as it had been observed in the case of Stephen in chapter 7. However, at this point my interest lies in highlighting the fact that Philip is just another one of the examples and by no means a unique case. Let's see.

The text that introduces the figure of Philip in chapter 8 is verse 4, which expresses the following: "Therefore, those who had been scattered went about preaching the word."

And immediately, as an example, the case of Philip is mentioned: "Philip went down to the city of Samaria and began proclaiming Christ to them" (v. 5).

Do you see what I mean? Philip is not a unique case; he is just one example among many, perhaps thousands. All who were scattered went everywhere preaching the gospel. "Everyone," not just Philip; "Everywhere," not only in Samaria but also in Galilee and throughout Judea, they went preaching the gospel. This is as extraordinary as the case of Philip himself, or perhaps more so.

Let's consider this for a moment. Overnight, thousands of brothers left their homes and their jobs to escape persecution. The cruelty of the persecution was of such magnitude that, literally, they escaped for their lives. Despite the seriousness of the situation, Luke expresses that this did not constitute an obstacle—rather that while the disciples fled, they evangelized everywhere they went. This deserves a hallelujah! Had you been in their place, would you have been concerned with proclaiming the gospel or escaping with your life? Shamefully, I must admit that, in my case, the latter would be true. Wherever you went, would you rush to present yourself as a Christian, or, for your own safety, would you try to go unnoticed?

It seems, then, that Stephen was not an exceptional case; neither was Philip. Here was a weight of glory that had spread throughout the entire church in Jerusalem. After three and a half years of maturation, the whole church had arrived at the stature of Christ. How do we know? Because the test of the persecution proved it.

Rubén I. Chacón

ONE WHO TRAVELS THE WAY OF THE CROSS

While the writer Luke, from chapter 8 to chapter 12 of the book of Acts, gives an account of the expansion of the church and the kingdom of God throughout Palestine, beginning with chapter 13, in parallel and simultaneously he sets the stage to present the testimony of the recently appointed apostle Paul.

In effect, in chapters 8–12 the author not only shows Saul's relationship with the death of Stephen and with the persecution in general that ravaged the church but also gives an account of the miraculous conversion experienced by this staunch persecutor. In addition, he presents in these chapters the record of how some of those "scattered" because of the persecution of Stephen arrived with the gospel beyond the borders of Israel to the city of Antioch in Syria. This place will be of great importance, not only because Barnabas will bring Saul of Tarsus to work with him for a whole year with the church in Antioch, but especially because this place and this church will be the operational center for apostle Paul's ministry. Paul will maintain a relationship with Antioch like the relationship the twelve have with Jerusalem. And it is from here, starting from the thirteenth chapter of Acts, that we will see Paul living like Christ in following after the way of the cross.

According to Luke, Christ's earthly life can be divided into three parts: (1) thirty years, (2) three years, and (3) six months. Luke dedicates the first three chapters of his gospel to the first thirty years of Jesus's life.[8] Luke dedicates the next six chapters of his gospel—chapters 4–9—to the second stage of Christ's life, which lasted three years and corresponds to his ministry. But to the last stage, which lasted only six months, Luke will dedicate the remaining fifteen chapters. This fact is striking: Three chapters for thirty years; six chapters for three years, and fifteen chapters for six months. Luke dedicates more attention to the shortest stage of Jesus's life. Why? Simply because, for Luke, this constituted the most important stage of his life.

Indeed, in this last stage, which begins "when the days were approaching for His ascension" (9:51), our blessed Lord began his last journey to Jerusalem, which could perfectly be called "the way of the cross," because on this occasion he would encounter death in Jerusalem. According to Luke 9, on the Mount of Transfiguration, where the second stage of Jesus's life ended, he discussed with Moses and Elijah his departure for Jerusalem (9:31). Therefore, the way of the cross goes from the Mount of Transfiguration to Mount Calvary. From mount to mount. From glory to death.

This is the most important stage in Jesus's life, because without the cross there is no redemption; without his death, there is no salvation. His three-year ministry was extraordinary. As someone said, he did in three years what all of us could not do in one thousand years. However, nothing done by Christ at this stage would have eternal saving value without his death on the cross. What finally brought us salvation was not his miracles, or his healings, or his teachings, but his redemptive death. Without the shedding of his blood on the cross of Calvary, there would have been no remission of sins.[9]

Therefore, Luke, whose purpose it was to present Jesus as the Son of Man who brought salvation to all men and to all kinds of men, paid greater attention precisely to the fundamental fact of our salvation: the way to expiatory death. This journey, which will cover the last six months of Jesus's life, will include the trip from Caesarea Philippi, in northern Israel, to Jerusalem in Judea, in southern Israel.

Now, the way of the cross that the Lord had to travel for our salvation was not only intended for him. It is also the path all his disciples will travel. Surely for most of us it will not be a literal and physical road as in the case of Christ; however, it is the path that we all must travel spiritually, since we are all called to be Christlike. This was made clear by the Lord himself in Luke 9:21–26.

But let's go back to Paul. Interestingly, Paul's Christian life can also be divided into three stages: in this case, eleven years each. In the first eleven years, where he did not make any apostolic journeys or write any letters, Paul, like all Pentecostal believers, first knew failure. As we have already seen, he learned to wait and walk in the Spirit. The second eleven years, as in the case of Christ, correspond to the time of his ministry, a fruitful ministry, during which he evangelized, planted churches, wrote several epistles, and trained workers. This second stage of Paul's Christian life is covered in the book of Acts from chapter 13 to chapter 20. From chapter 20 on, Paul, like Christ, will also undertake one last journey to Jerusalem that will mean spending practically the last eleven years of his life in prison and finally encountering death, approximately in the year 67 AD. For

Paul, this "obligatory" path constitutes his own way of the cross, where in some small measure, the way of the cross traveled by his own Lord will be reproduced in his life, by the Spirit.

On his first apostolic journey, Paul specifically traveled through the region of Galatia, where he had planted at least four churches: Antioch of Pisidia, Iconium, Lystra, and Derbe (see Acts 13–14). On his second apostolic journey, he toured the regions of Macedonia (Philippi, Thessalonica, and Berea) and Achaia (Athens and Corinth). This journey is covered in chapters 15–18 of Acts. On Paul's third trip, he mainly toured the region of Asia and particularly the city of Ephesus, where he settled for about three years (20:31). From here and through his collaborators, he evangelized all of Asia, and God performed extraordinary miracles by Paul's hand (19:10–11). Definitely, this is where Paul lives the climax of his ministry.

From the city of Ephesus, Paul also wrote the noteworthy first letter to the Corinthians, in which he said that he would be in Ephesus until Pentecost.[10] Ephesus, without a doubt, represented "Pentecost" in Paul's ministry. Luke sums up Paul's ministry at Ephesus in these words: "the word of the Lord spread widely and grew in power" (19:20).

However, and this is the amazing thing, Paul, amid so much glory, resolved in the Spirit to go to Jerusalem (19:21). It was as if Paul, on his own mount of transfiguration (Ephesus), sensed that his ministry was culminating and that the time had come, as in the case of his Master, to head toward Jerusalem. In the case of Christ, Luke says that when the time for his ascension was come, "he set his face to go to Jerusalem." In Paul's case, Luke puts it this way: "Now after these things were finished, Paul proposed in the Spirit to go to Jerusalem" (19: 21).
Thanks to the Gospel of John, we know that Jesus, during his earthly ministry, went up to Jerusalem three times—the last time, to be crucified.[11] Paul, during his apostolic ministry (Acts 13 onward), like his Master, also went up to Jerusalem three times, as Luke testifies in Acts. The last time, he also was willing to die.

The first time that Paul went up to Jerusalem in his capacity as an apostle of Jesus Christ was when he attended the Council of Jerusalem (15). The second time was when, returning from his second apostolic trip, he did not want to stay longer in Ephesus, because he wanted to observe a Jewish holiday in Jerusalem.[12] The expression "went up to greet the church" in 18:22 refers, in effect, to the church in Jerusalem.

The third time, as in the case of his Lord, would be the last, and it was to this occasion that the text of 19:21 refers.

But what motivates Paul to leave the "glory" of Ephesus to make this trip to Jerusalem? In the immediate and more superficial sense, Paul has proposed to take an offering from the Gentile churches to the saints in Jerusalem. However, this is the "excuse," a spiritual excuse, without a doubt. In his letter to the Philippians, however, he reveals the true reason for his trip to Jerusalem. There, he says:

> I count all things to be loss in view of the surpassing value of knowing Christ Jesus my Lord, for whom I have suffered the loss of all things, and count them but rubbish so that I may gain Christ
>
> … that I may know Him and the power of His resurrection and the fellowship of His sufferings, being conformed to His death. (3:8, 10)

According to his own testimony, Paul's highest objective in life was to know Christ. And for this he longed to participate in the sufferings of Christ and to become like him in his death. According to Luke, Paul is bound by the Spirit to do so (20:22). He is a "slave" to this purpose. The NIV puts it this way: "And now, compelled by the Spirit, I am going to Jerusalem."

Now then, a not-so-small disturbance that occurred in Ephesus indicated to Paul that the time to undertake the journey had arrived (19:23–41). His itinerary, due to the offerings Paul was collecting, would be the regions of Macedonia and Achaia. And indeed, after passing through the Macedonian region, he arrived in Greece, specifically the city of Corinth, where he settled, as he had planned, for three months (20:2–3).[13] From there he wrote the important epistle to the Romans, where he tells them of his trip to Jerusalem and the reason for it:

Now, I am going to Jerusalem serving the saints. For Macedonia and Achaia have been pleased to make a contribution for the poor among the saints in Jerusalem. Yes, they were pleased to do so, and they are indebted to them. For if the Gentiles have shared in their spiritual things, they are indebted to minister to them also in material things. Therefore, when I have finished this, and have put my seal on this fruit of theirs, I will go on by way of you to Spain. I know that when I come to you, I will come in the fullness of the blessing of Christ.

Now I urge you, brethren, by our Lord Jesus Christ and by the love of the Spirit, to strive together with me in your prayers to God for me, that I may be rescued from those who are disobedient in Judea, and that my service for Jerusalem may prove acceptable to the saints; so that I may come to you in joy by the will of God and find refreshing rest in your company. Now the God of peace be with you all. Amen. (Romans 15:25–33)

In this letter, Paul expresses his desire to reach Rome, and even Spain. However, he senses that his visit to Jerusalem will not be easy, so he requests the prayer of the Romans so that he may joyfully arrive in Rome by God's will. Could Paul have understood that his arrival in Rome would be in chains?

From Corinth, according to the original plan, Paul intended to go to Syria and from there to Jerusalem. But, upon discovering a plan of the Jews to assassinate him, he changes his itinerary and decides to return to Macedonia and Asia. The itinerary would then be the following: (1) Philippi (20:6), (2) Troas (20:7–12), (3) Miletus (20:13–38), (4) Tyre (21:1–6), (5) Ptolemaide (21:7), (6) Caesarea (21:8–14), and (7) Jerusalem (21:15, 23:22). Seven places in total.

In the case of Jesus, Luke barely mentions the places that serve as a stopover on the journey that Christ makes from Caesarea Philippi to Jerusalem. The reason lies in the fact that Luke wants to emphasize the journey itself. Luke's account highlights not the places Jesus visits along the way but where he is going, where he is heading. Therefore, even though he hardly gives the names of the places through which Jesus passes, nevertheless, seven times he mentions that he is heading to Jerusalem:

1. "When the days were approaching for His ascension, He was determined to go to Jerusalem" (Luke 9:51).
2. "And He was passing through from one city and village to another, teaching, and proceeding on His way to Jerusalem" (Luke 13:22).
3. "Nevertheless I must journey on today and tomorrow and the next day; for it cannot be that a prophet would perish outside of Jerusalem" (Luke 13:33).
4. "While He was on the way to Jerusalem, He was passing between Samaria and Galilee" (Luke 17:11).
5. "Then He took the twelve aside and said to them, "Behold, we are going up to Jerusalem, and all things which are written through the prophets about the Son of Man will be accomplished" (Luke 18:31).
6. "While they were listening to these things, Jesus went on to tell a parable, because He was near Jerusalem, and they supposed that the kingdom of God was going to appear immediately" (Luke 19:11).
7. "After He had said these things, He was going on ahead, going up to Jerusalem" (Luke 19:28).

But let's go back to Paul. In Asia he passes through Troas and Miletus. He does not want to go through Ephesus to get to Jerusalem for the day of Pentecost (20:16). It is his longing to have a "Pentecost" also in Jerusalem.

In Miletus he calls the elders of the church in Ephesus and solemnly bids them farewell, because never again will they see his face. But are these premonitions well founded? Yes. In his address to the elders, Paul states that the Holy Spirit has born witness to him in all cities, telling him that in Jerusalem prisons and tribulations await him. So why does he go? We already know that the reason goes beyond the issue of the presentation of the offerings.

From Miletus he went to Tyre, in the region of Syria, where he stayed with the brothers for seven days. There, the brothers, led by the Spirit, asked him not to go up to Jerusalem. It was the second time that Luke recorded the warnings given to Paul by the Spirit.

From Tyre, Paul arrived at Ptolemais, where he stayed one day with the brothers. Then he continued to Caesarea where he spent a few days at the home of Philip, the evangelist. While there, a prophet named Agabus came down from Judea, who, taking Paul's belt and tying his own hands and feet, said:

> This is what the Holy Spirit says: "In this way the Jews
> at Jerusalem will bind the man who owns this belt and
> deliver him into the hands of the Gentiles. (Acts 21:11)

This was the third and last time that Luke records what was spoken by the Spirit regarding Paul's journey to Jerusalem, just as his Master had warned his disciples three times regarding his death in Jerusalem. All of this happened, in both cases, while they were on their way to the city of Jerusalem.[14]

But the similarities don't end here. Luke says that upon hearing Agabus's prophecy:

> We as well as the local residents began begging him not
> to go up to Jerusalem. Then Paul answered, "What are
> you doing, weeping and breaking my heart? For I am
> ready not only to be bound, but even to die at Jerusalem
> for the name of the Lord Jesus." And since he would not
> be persuaded, we fell silent, remarking, "The will of the
> Lord be done!" (Acts 21:12–14).

Does this scene sound familiar to you? To which other is it similar? To the scene when Jesus first spoke of his death to the disciples. Do you remember? (See Mark 8:31–38). Let's look at some of the details here:

First, Luke says that not only did the local people ask him not to go up to Jerusalem, but also "we beg you," Luke records. To whom does Luke refer when he uses the expression *we*? What happened is that Paul, like his Lord, was not going to Jerusalem alone. He was also accompanied by "his" disciples. Not only was Luke with him as evidenced by using the first-person plural (we); he was also accompanied by Trophimus (21:29),

Aristarchus (27:2), and probably others (20:4). It would not surprise me if in total there had been about twelve companions.

Second, the fact that his own fellow laborers asked him not to go up to Jerusalem reminds us of Peter trying to dissuade the Lord:

> And He began to teach them that the Son of Man must suffer many things and be rejected by the elders and the chief priests and the scribes, and be killed, and after three days rise again. And He was stating the matter plainly. And Peter took Him aside and began to rebuke Him. (Mark 8:31–32).

As for Paul, his reaction reminds us of Jesus's own reaction:

> But turning around and seeing His disciples, He rebuked Peter and said, "Get behind Me, Satan; for you are not setting your mind on God's interests, but man's." (Mark 8:33)

I hope you can grasp that what Luke is showing us here is not simple similarities between Christ and Paul, but rather how Christ's life is reproduced in the lives of his disciples through the Holy Spirit. What we have here is Christ being made manifest through his church. The same Christ of the gospel now being replicated by the Spirit. The same Christ and his same works.

Third, when Paul entered Jerusalem, he was accompanied, in addition to his fellow laborers, by other brothers, just as in the case of Jesus (21:15–16).[15]

When he finally arrived in Jerusalem, the reception was very warm, like the one that had been offered to their Lord (21:17). But once in Jerusalem, while Paul was fulfilling a vow in the temple, some Jews from Asia agitated the entire crowd and laid hands on him. The accusations seem an echo of those made against Christ and Stephen: "This is the man who preaches to all men everywhere against our people and the law and this place" (21:28). And like they had done to his Savior, the crowds shouted, "Die!"[16] As was the case with his Master, and the twelve and Stephen, he was arrested and had to appear before the Jewish Council (22:30–23:11). Paul had just started his defense when the high priest, Ananias, ordered those next to him to strike him on the mouth (23:1–2).

The same had happened to his Master when he appeared before the high priest Ananias, Caiaphas's father-in-law.[17]

Paul, the next day, was to appear for the second time before the council. However, being warned of a plot against him, he ended up being taken by the Gentile authorities to a prison in Caesarea, where he would finally spend two years incarcerated (24:27).

And so ends Paul's ascent to Jerusalem, his own version of the "way of the cross." Although, unlike his Lord, Paul did not experience physical death in Jerusalem, nevertheless, just because he was willing to go to Jerusalem, despite the Spirit's warnings, we can say without a doubt that, like his Lord, Paul journeyed toward his death. Had you been in Paul's place, would you have gone?

Indeed, Paul was not only willing to suffer, but to die for his Lord. His words about it were very clear:

> And now, behold, bound by the Spirit, I am on my way to Jerusalem, not knowing what will happen to me there, except that the Holy Spirit solemnly testifies to me in every city, saying that bonds and afflictions await me. But I do not consider my life of any account as dear to myself, so that I may finish my course and the ministry which I received from the Lord Jesus, to testify solemnly of the gospel of the grace of God. (Acts 20:22–24)

> When we had heard this, we as well as the local residents began begging him not to go up to Jerusalem. Then Paul answered, "What are you doing, weeping and breaking my heart? For I am ready not only to be bound, but even to die at Jerusalem for the name of the Lord Jesus." And since he would not be persuaded, we fell silent, remarking, "The will of the Lord be done." (Acts 21:12–14)

Paul's life journey included traveling the way of the cross, which he did, experiencing it spiritually. But since Paul did not experience death physically, one wonders what the benefit of having taken that route was? Well, we said earlier that Paul's Christian life could be divided into three stages of eleven years each. We also said that the second stage, that of his ministry, culminated in Ephesus. The last stage, therefore, begins with the trip to Jerusalem, where he is arrested and spends two years in prison. But the book of Acts doesn't end there. After two years in prison in Caesarea, Paul was taken in chains to Rome to appear before Caesar himself (27–28). And according to Luke's own testimony, Paul stayed in Rome for two whole years in a rented house (28:30).

So, of the last eleven years of Paul's life, the book of Acts accounts for only the first four years. However, the relevant fact is that Paul spent those four years in prison. Therefore, the question arises: If Paul, although having experienced the way of the cross spiritually, nevertheless continued living, of what value was it then to have taken the way of the cross? Of great value. From prison in Rome, apostle Paul wrote four epistles commonly known as the Christology Epistles: Ephesians, Colossians, Philippians, and Philemon.

What is surprising about this fact is that in these letters, Paul reached the ultimate level of revelation. That is, the more confined Paul was, the higher he scaled in revelation. Descending to the lowest point, he rose to the greatest heights.

The way of the cross is, then, the way of revelation. At least that was so in Paul's case. So, we thank the Lord Jesus Christ for the great blessing that Paul bequeathed to all future generations of Christians. This way of the cross has been immensely more profitable for God's work than if Paul had continued preaching and planting churches. Blessed and precious are the ways of God!

1 According to the short chronological record, this process also took three and a half years.

2 In fact, it is likely that these were the same people that condemned Jesus.

3 As an example, see John 18:19–24.

4 Compare Matthew 26:.47, Luke 22:47, John 18:3.

5 Compare Matthew 26:59–60, Mark 14:55–56.

6 Reference here is to the most relevant aspect but not the only one.

7 It is only in the collective sense that we obtain the fullness of the image of Christ (Ephesians 4:13).

8 See Luke 3:23.

9 Ref. Hebrews 9:22.

10 See 1 Corinthians 16:8.

11 See John 2:13, 23; 6:4; 11:55.

12 Perhaps as part or the culmination of the vow take in Cencrea (18:18).

13 Compare 1 Corinthians 16:5–7.

14 See Luke 9:22, 44; 18:31–33.

15 Compare Mark 15:40–41, Luke 23:49.

16 Compare Luke 23:21.

17 Compare John 18:19–23.

CONCLUSION

The victorious Christian life does not consist of a personal relationship with Christ in which a kind of collaboration percentage exists from both parties. For example, we do 50 percent of the work, and the Lord does the other 50 percent. Nor does it work like this, that the Lord does 80 percent and we 20 percent. It doesn't work that way, not even in the hypothetical case that the Lord does 99 percent and us only 1 percent. No, the victorious Christian life is still something more extraordinary than all that. Rather, it is Christ, through the Holy Spirit, who does it all, 100 percent, through us. Our participation in the relationship and communion with the Lord does not consist, then, in helping the Lord Jesus Christ not even to some small degree; much less does it consist of him helping us, not even a little.

No, our participation in the victorious Christian life consists of being open channels, through which the life of Christ, by the Spirit, flows freely in us and through us, without opposition or resistance from our inner self or soul. Since this is not a natural condition for us due to the reality of sin, our inner self or soul must be broken to be redeemed.

The Lord does not seek to destroy or annihilate our inner self, or even to nullify it. The good news of the gospel is that in Christ we are redeemed, not destroyed. But for this to happen, our soul must be broken so that it returns to the original condition that the Lord intended for it, and thus becomes a docile and sensitive instrument of the spirit.

Now, the divine method by which we are broken, according to the discipleship of Jesus, is none other than being made to drink the dust of defeat until we give up on ourselves and surrender completely to the Lord and his Spirit. The divine methodology does not consist simply in failing, but in the fact that when we are defeated, we are brought into absolute and permanent dependence on Christ. As Paul put it: "Therefore the Law has become our tutor to lead us to Christ, so that we may be justified by faith" (Galatians 3:24).

When the Lord's dealings gradually forge in us, little by little, this spiritual condition necessary for a victorious life, we get closer and closer to the blessed reality of which Christ is the perfect and absolute paradigm: "Truly, truly, I say to you, the Son can do nothing of Himself" (John 5:19).

By this means, our service to the Lord begins to become a service that is free from the sweat of the flesh.

SERVICE WITHOUT SWEAT

> They shall enter my sanctuary; they shall come near to my table to minister to me and keep my charge. It shall be that when they enter at the gates of the inner court, they shall be clothed with linen garments; and wool shall not be on them while they are ministering in the gates of the inner court and in the house. Linen turbans shall be on their heads and linen undergarments shall be on their loins; they shall not gird themselves with anything which makes them sweat." (Ezekiel 44:16–18)

This is an ordinance for the Lord's priests. In the new covenant, we are all priests, and we can all enter the sanctuary and minister to God. This ordinance of the Lord states that the priests must enter dressed in linen garments. They shall not wear anything made of wool. The reason why they shouldn't wear woolen clothing, according to verse 18, is so their clothes won't make them sweat.

"They won't wear anything that makes them sweat." This means that God does not want "sweat" in his house. What does sweat mean? Sweat occurs when we exert energy. Therefore, sweat represents human effort. If God does not want "sweat" in his house, it means that God does not want human effort in his house. Interesting, don't you think?

Let's now read Leviticus 19:19: "You are to keep my statutes. You shall not breed together two kinds of your cattle; you shall not sow your field with mixed seeds, nor wear a garment upon you of two kinds of material mixed together."

"You shall not sow your field with mixed seeds." Let's emphasize the word *mixed*. "And you will not wear clothes with mixed threads." Again, let's emphasize the word *mixed*. God does not want a mixture of linen and wool. God does not want a mixture of the divine with the human. Human effort in God's house hinders God's work.

God doesn't want us to perform 50 percent and let him do the other 50 percent, nor for us to do 10 percent and let him do 90 percent. He wants to do it all—100 percent. It is very difficult for us to understand that our growth in the Lord comes as we diminish, so that the Lord may increase. The Lord wants to make room in us, so that he can do it all.

You have read the letter to the Galatians. The Galatians were falling into this same error. They had been justified by faith; they had been saved by faith, but now they believed that sanctification was by works. And Paul comes to tell them: "No, sanctification is also by faith." Everything is by faith; everything is the work of God.

God's work is his work—100 percent. He doesn't need our help; he doesn't need our intrusion. We simply need to be available, be open, and allow the Lord to do his complete work. God's work is perfect, God's work is absolute; it is a finished work, and it is an eternal work. Praise the Lord! May the Father open our eyes to see that we are contemplating a work that is already finished.

THE PURPOSE OF GOD

Why doesn't God want our efforts? To know the answer, we need to understand how we were created and for what we were created. In other words, we need to know God's purpose. And when we delve into God's purpose, we find that you and I were created to contain Christ and to express Christ, so that the life of Christ would be manifested through us.

Therefore, from the beginning, God never designed us in a way that we had to help God. From the beginning, he created and designed us as a vessel to contain the life of Christ, and for that life to be manifest through us.

It is not, therefore, because we have sinned that we cannot offer anything acceptable to God. It is not only sin, which has stained all that we do, that makes our actions hybrid or mixed, but there is an even deeper reason. We were never created to help God, but rather to let him manifest himself through us.

God's plan was as follows: Man was created tripartite (i.e., spirit, soul, and body). Adam was created with human life. As the scripture says, he was made a "living soul." However, he was created for the tree of life. He was created with one kind of life—human life—but he was created for another kind of life: the life that came from the tree of life.

So, when God created Adam, he put him in the garden, and in the middle of the garden, God planted the tree of life and the tree of the knowledge of good and evil. Adam was made by the creative hand of God with human life, but he was created to access that life that was in the tree of life.

What life was there for Adam in the tree of life if he had already been created with human life? The life that is in the tree of life is the life of Christ. And God's purpose was that Adam, created with will, with intellect, and with emotions, would voluntarily agree to eat from the tree of life. When Adam went to the center of the garden, even though the tree of the knowledge of good and evil was there, from which Adam was not to eat, there was also the tree of life.

When Adam ventured to the center of the garden, he should have eaten from that tree. If Adam had done that, the life of God, which is the life of Christ, would have entered his spirit, and in his spirit, he would have had the life of Christ. Then, Adam, from that moment, could have expressed the life of the Lord. The life of Christ would have begun to be manifest through him. His soul would have been in harmony with his spirit, and the soul, like a wife, would have been the spirit's helpmeet; the spirit would have been like the husband, and the soul like the wife. And the soul, which had no sin, would follow the spirit without resistance and without opposition. Man would then have been an expression of Christ. Man would not have expressed himself but Christ.

Now, we all know that this did not happen. Sadly, Adam disobeyed. When he went to the center of the garden, he ate from the tree of the knowledge of good and evil. And God said: "Let him not now reach out his hand and eat from the tree of life as well." His spirit did not receive life from God, and this drama ensued: the soul prevailed over the spirit.

Instead of being a servant, the soul became the queen. Instead of being a wife, she became a husband, and began to live for herself. She became self-sufficient, autonomous, rebellious, and hyperactive. She strengthened her capabilities. The will became an iron will. The mind, a mind that intellectualized everything. Her feelings became unbalanced, dragging her this way and that. The soul went astray, left its place, put itself in a position for which it was never created.

Therefore, God does not want our human effort in his house. God wants the original plan: the spirit of man made alive with divine life and expressing itself through a docile soul—a soul that is a servant of the spirit, a soul that does not resist what is of God, and that can follow in a tangible way what the life of Christ wants to express.

But from the day Adam sinned, man has expressed himself. What comes out of us is not the expression of Christ; rather it is the expression of ourselves. What is of human origin comes into God's house, and in the house of God there appears a mixture. On the one hand, there is Christ, who sometimes flows and manifests himself, yet there is still a lot of humanness in the house of God.

THE ACTIVISM OF THE SOUL

Not only do we have a soul that is out of place, in a position for which it was never created, but this hyperactivity in which the soul is engaged, this autonomy that it exercises, this force with which it wants to perform, finally produces fatigue, produces sweat, produces a worn-out soul, which when it sweats to please God, to serve God, it experiences neither joy nor rest. On the contrary, human effort brings with it complaints, discouragement, frustration, depression, and dissatisfaction.

How many of us are tired, exhausted, frustrated, and discouraged! God does not want sweat in his house. God wants his service, the service offered to him, to be done with joy, be done with peace, be done with rest and with happiness. We need the rest of the Lord; we need to put our soul at ease, and let the Lord work through us.

Isaiah 57:10 says: "In the multitude of your ways you were tired, but you did not say: There is no remedy; you found new vigor in your hand, therefore you were not discouraged." This is the situation of our soul.

Going many directions, seeking to participate, seeking fulfillment, seeking to collaborate, trying to help God.

In other words, our ways tire us out, but not to the point of saying, "There is no more hope." Our soul regains vigor, is filled with hope again, and is not discouraged and continues. And all over again, we get tired, and we get frustrated, but not to the point of saying, "There is no remedy." Rather, we take on renewed energy, and we defer discouragement. This is not what the Lord wants. The Lord wants us to get to the point of total surrender.

Verse 20 says: "But the ungodly are like the stormy sea, which cannot be stilled." So is the soul of man like the sea in a storm, which cannot be still. And verse 21 says: "There is no peace, said my God, for the ungodly."

REST FOR THE SOUL

Jeremiah 6:16 says: "Thus says the LORD, 'Stand by the ways and see and ask for the ancient paths, where the good way is, and walk in it. And you will find rest for your souls.'"

"Stand by the ways." The word *ways* is plural. Isaiah had said: "In the multitude of your ways you were weary." That is the soul's problem. It travels along a multitude of roads. And the prophet Jeremiah says: "Stand by the ways and see and ask for the ancient paths, where the good way is." In the singular, there is only one way.

There are not many ways; there is only one way—the good way. And the prophet says that when you find it, walk in it, "and you will find rest for your soul." When we look at the fulfillment of this in the New Testament, we read in Matthew 11:28–30: "Come to me, all you who are weary and heavy-laden, and I will give you rest. Take my yoke upon you and learn from me, for I am meek and humble in heart; and you will find rest for your souls. For my yoke it is easy, and my burden is light."

Is there someone who is working and who is oppressed? "Come to me," says Christ, "you who are weary and heavy-laden, and I will give you rest." How does the Lord give us rest? "Take my yoke upon you …" That is to say, that our soul return to its original position, cease to be self-sufficient, cease to be autonomous. That our soul once again submit to the spirit. The yoke of Christ upon us is his spirit.

And the Lord says, "and learn from me, for I am meek and humble of heart; and you will find rest for your souls." He took this quote from Jeremiah chapter 6. Therefore, according to the Lord himself, who is the good way? He himself was the good way. Christ is the good way. And by bearing his yoke, we find rest for our souls, because the yoke of Christ is easy, and his burden is light.

We find rest and quietness, we regain joy and happiness, sweat disappears, when we have yoked ourselves to Christ—when we learn to walk with him, when we let him go before us, when we allow him to do 100 percent of the effort, when we decrease so that he can increase so that he can fill everything in his house, so that we can once again become his servants; we can once again be docile to his Spirit.

And finally, 2 Timothy 2:1: "You therefore, my son, be strong in the grace that is in Christ Jesus." It seems there is a contradiction here. Paul says to Timothy, "Be strong." So, what's it going to be? Should we make an effort, or should we not make an effort? If we look closely, Paul says to Timothy: "Be strong in the grace." It does not say, "be strong in the flesh." And this is a paradox because grace is the opposite of works. So, the verb "be strong" seems to have no relation to grace. But Paul says to Timothy: "Be strong," yes, but "in the grace that is in Christ Jesus."

To paraphrase this text, it would read more or less like this: "Make an effort to do nothing in the flesh; strive to let God do everything." And why does doing nothing require effort? Because our soul is all too ready to do something; our soul is always ready to take the initiative. Our soul cannot be still.

What is our biggest problem when we pray? We possess a soul that cannot be still or silent. That's the way it is. As soon as we want to settle in the presence of God, we feel and experience that our soul is active, full of ideas, full of good intentions. And as soon as we try to be still, we discover that we cannot. We need to try to do nothing, because our natural tendency is always to do something.

So, this text does not contradict what we have said; rather, it is a paradox. Try to do nothing yourself; strive for God to do everything. God can do 100 percent, and He wants to do it through you, without sweat, without fatigue, without complaints, without frustration, without discouragement, but with joy, with gladness, in the rest of the Lord. Amen.